Contributions
to American
Anthropology
and History

No. 60

PREHISTORIC CERAMICS AND SETTLEMENT PATTERNS IN QUINTANA ROO, MEXICO

WILLIAM T. SANDERS

Issued 1960

With nineteen figures and a frontispiece

Manuscript submitted December 1957

The Kirby Lithographic Company, Inc., Washington, D. C.

The Meriden Gravure Company, Meriden, Connecticut

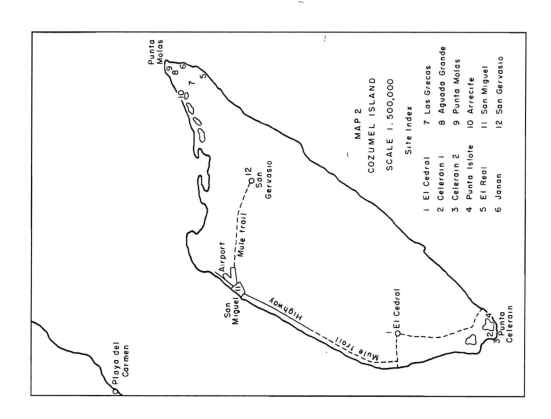

MAP 2

COZUMEL ISLAND

SCALE 1.500,000

Site Index

1 El Cedral   7 Los Grecas
2 Celerain I   8 Aguada Grande
3 Celerain 2   9 Punta Molas
4 Punta Islote   10 Arrecife
5 El Real   11 San Miguel
6 Janan   12 San Gervasio

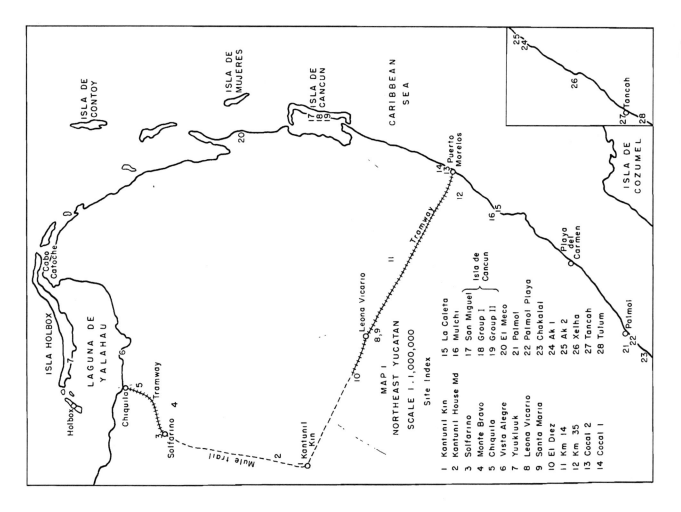

MAP I

NORTHEAST YUCATAN

SCALE I:1,000,000

Site Index

1 Kantunil Kin   15 La Caleta
2 Kantunil House Md   16 Mulchi
3 Solfarino   17 San Miguel ⎫
4 Monte Bravo   18 Group I   ⎬ Isla de
5 Chiquila   19 Group II   ⎭ Cancun
6 Vista Alegre   20 El Meco
7 Yuukluuk   21 Palmol
8 Leona Vicario   22 Palmol Playa
9 Santa Maria   23 Chakalal
10 El Diez   24 Ak I
11 Km 14   25 Ak 2
12 Km 35   26 Xelha
13 Cocal 2   27 Tancah
14 Cocal I   28 Tulum

CONTENTS

1. INTRODUCTION 161
2. TANCAH—EXCAVATIONS AND CERAMIC ANALYSIS 162
   General description 162
   Excavations 163
      Group A stratigraphic trenches 163
      Group B stratigraphic trenches 166
      Miscellaneous stratigraphic trenches 167
   Ceramic chronology at Tancah 169
      Introduction 169
      Group A 169
      Group B 171
      Settlement-pattern trenches 174
3. TULUM—EXCAVATIONS AND CERAMIC ANALYSIS 175
   General description 175
   Excavations 177
   Ceramic chronology of Tulum 183
4. NORTHERN QUINTANA ROO 189
   North-coast sites 189
   Cozumel Island sites 193
   East-coast sites 197
   Interior sites 199
5. CHETUMAL AREA 203
   Ichpaatun 203
   Calderitas 207
6. SETTLEMENT PATTERNS 209
   Tancah 209
   Tulum 212
   Miscellaneous site patterns 218
7. CHRONOLOGY IN QUINTANA ROO 220
   Tulum-Tancah area 220
   Other east-coast sites 221
   North coast 222
   Cozumel Island 223
   Interior sites 224
   The ceramic column for northern Quintana Roo 225
   Architecture 227
8. QUINTANA ROO AND THE LOWLAND MAYA AREA 228
   Tulum Period wares 228
   Vista Alegre complex 231
   San Miguel complex 231
   Regional Polychrome 232
   Tancah complex 233
   Chetumal area pottery 235
9. APPENDIX A—POTTERY WARES 237
   Tulum Complex Wares 237
      Tulum Red ware 237
      Tulum Plain ware 243
      Fine Orange 244
      Mayapan Black-on-Cream 244
      Censer wares 245

9. APPENDIX A—POTTERY WARES—continued
   Vista Alegre-San Miguel Complex Wares   248
      Vista Alegre Striated   248
      Yucatan Slate ware   249
      Yucatan Thin Slate   250
   Tancah Complex Wares   250
      Late Formative Monochrome   250
      Tancah Plain-Tancah Striated   252
   Regional Polychrome.   254
   Chetumal Area Classic Wares.   255
      Calderitas Striated   255
      Calderitas Fine Paste Striated   255
      Calderitas Red   256
      Calderitas Polychrome   256
      Calderitas Polished Black   257
      Calderitas Heavy Plain   257
10. APPENDIX B—ARCHITECTURE.   258
   Tancah.   258
   Ichpaatun   260
11. APPENDIX C—MISCELLANEOUS ARTIFACTS   261
12. REFERENCES   263

ILLUSTRATIONS

Frontispiece — Maps of northeastern Yucatan and Cozumel Island,
showing archaeological sites visited.

Figures at end of text

Fig. 1 — Map of Tancah.

Fig. 2 — Map of Tulum.

Fig. 3 — Building plans and site profiles.

Fig. 4 — Tulum Red bowls.

Fig. 5 — Tulum Red jars and rare forms.

Fig. 6 — Tulum Red and Tulum Plain wares.

Fig. 7 — Tulum Period wares.

Fig. 8 — Tulum Period censer wares.

Fig. 9 — Vista Alegre Striated and Tancah Period wares.

Fig. 10 — Tancah Period wares and Regional Polychrome.

Fig. 11 — Yucatan Slate, Chetumal area wares, and unclassified pottery.

Fig. 12 — Architecture.

Fig. 13 — Architecture, burial, and general views.

Fig. 14 — Architecture.

Fig. 15 — Pottery vessels from various sites.

Fig. 16 — Fragments of Tulum Period censer wares.

Fig. 17 — Animal and human effigies, and tubular handled censers.

Fig. 18 — Tulum Period pottery.

Fig. 19 — Artifacts of stone and shell.

CHARTS

Chart 1 — Frequencies of wares from stratigraphic trenches at
Tancah 170
Chart 2 — Frequencies of wares from settlement-pattern trenches
at Tancah 173
Chart 3 — Ceramic chronology of Quintana Roo 226

TABLES

Table 1 — Building stratigraphy at Tulum 185
Table 2 — Frequencies of wares and shapes from stratigraphic
trenches at Tulum 187
Table 3 — Frequencies of wares and shapes (post-Classic) from
trenches at Ichpaatun 205
Table 4 — Settlement-pattern trenches at Tulum 214

1. INTRODUCTION

On the basis of Spanish accounts one of the most important areas of lowland Mesoamerica at the time of the Conquest was the east coast of Yucatan. Cozumel Island had replaced Chichen Itza as a pilgrimage center, and the regions around modern Chetumal and along the Laguna de Yalahau were evidently demographic and cultural centers of Yucatecan Maya civilization at that period.

Obviously, then, the area is of extreme importance for an understanding of the origin and character of post-Classic Maya culture. For this reason, in 1954 I conducted a survey of the northeast and east-central coast of the peninsula and of a part of the huge forested inland region north of Coba. Forty sites, some never before reported, others well established in the literature, were visited and roughly mapped; brief settlement-pattern surveys were made by limited trail cutting in the vicinity of the centers; and, finally, small trenches were dug to get ceramic samples for dating. The trenches were excavated mainly off the edges of constructions in shallow soil deposits. The soil was seldom deep enough for arbitrary stratigraphy, and building stratigraphy was attempted for only a few sites. In general, our samples may be characterized as excavated surface collections, if such a phrase is meaningful. At any rate, they perhaps provide a total occupational time range and less probably a mean date for a site. The chronological significance of the samples will be discussed in more detail in the text.

On the basis of the 1954 survey two of the largest sites on the coast, Tancah and Tulum, were selected for intensive testing in 1955. As they are major sites, and near each other, the possibility of working out a long, highly localized ceramic sequence seemed good. Lothrop's (1924) study had revealed striking and historically significant differences between them in architecture and in settlement patterns. When tested in 1954, Tulum samples seemed to be entirely of the post-Classic Period, whereas samples from Tancah suggested both a post-Classic and a Classic occupation. Everything, then, pointed to probable success in working out east-coast chronology on the basis of testing at the two places. The results fully justified our hopes and provided the key to dating the 1954 samples as well. Aside from chronology as indicated by ceramics, extensive surveying and trenching disclosed important data on settlement patterns at both sites.

After the work at Tulum and Tancah (12 weeks with 6 to 8 laborers), a week was spent in the vicinity of Chetumal on the southern border of Quintana Roo. The principal purpose of this survey was to test and date the ruins of Ichpaatun, described previously by Escalona Ramos (1946, pp. 522-530). This site is walled and has columned palaces similar to those at Tulum. It seemed, on architectural evidence, to be contemporary with Tulum, and verification of this dating by ceramic comparison was sought. Near Ichpaatun, another large site, called Calderitas by Escalona Ramos (1946, pp. 515-519), was also tested.

The ceramic collections, especially those from the 1955 season, were large, and time for complete study was limited to about 6 months. As this excursion into the complex world of ceramic typology is my first, I am perfectly aware of the general limitations and deficiencies of my ceramic analysis. Some of my typology may need revision. I especially may be accused by fellow archaeologists of too much "lumping" and not enough "hair splitting." On the other hand, the basic seriation of wares in Quintana Roo seems clear, and will, I believe, provide a useful chronological tool for working out the cultural history of the area. The most serious defect in the ceramic analysis was the lack of laboratory testing of tempering materials in the defined wares.

2. TANCAH — EXCAVATIONS AND CERAMIC ANALYSIS

GENERAL DESCRIPTION

Tancah is one of the largest of all ceremonial centers in Quintana Roo. It has been described in detail by Lothrop (1924, pp. 120-133), who mapped the two major groups, A and B, and described the individual structures in them. Group A consists of 11 structures around a somewhat trapezoidal-shaped plaza with the small end of the trapezoid to the east (fig. 1). The plaza is oriented almost due north, but not all the individual buildings are oriented exactly on this axis. If all the group were enclosed in a grid square, it would measure about 80 m north-south and 70 m east-west. The plaza is small, only about 40 m in its greatest dimension. The 11 surrounding structures, entirely religious in function, include 2 temples on high terraced pyramids, 2 others on high single terrace bases, 1 on a very low platform, 2 mounds of indefinite type, 3 altar-like platforms, and 1 low stone-walled enclosure. The only one of imposing size is Structure 1, which, being less than 7 m high from the top of the summit temple to the plaza floor and about 18 m square, is large only in comparison with others at the same site.

Group B, situated approximately 80 m southwest, includes 12 structures grouped around an elongated irregular plaza. In surface area and plaza size the group is similar to Group A. All these buildings too are religious in function, including 3 high pyramids with summit structures, 1 unclassifiable mound, 1 temple on a low platform, and 7 altar-like platforms. Again, all structures are small in comparison with those in other parts of the Maya area.

A preliminary survey made in 1954 revealed a large number of unmapped structures west and northwest of Groups A and B. One of the major tasks of the 1955 season was mapping them. As the area is covered by dense tropical jungle, trails were cut through the bush in a regular grid pattern to facilitate mapping and settlement-pattern excavations. Although the grid trails were laid off with a compass and do not pretend to be very accurate, surprisingly good results were obtained.

An area measuring 200 m east-west by 220 m north-south, which includes Groups A and B, was completely crisscrossed by trails on a 20-m grid. Alternate grid lines were extended to form an outer grid of 40-m squares, mainly to the north and west, where most of the unmapped structures lay. This extension of the grid system runs 40 m east of the inner grid, 80 m north, and 120 m west. It was not extended south, as that area was pasture and no structures were seen there. The total area covered by the 20- and 40-m grid squares, then, was 360 m east-west and 300 m north-south. It includes most of the constructions on the site except to the west.

Aside from the completely gridded area described, a few trails were extended farther into the bush for a distance of 120 m in all directions: five were cut north of the grid, one east, one south, and four west. Thus we had settlement-pattern data covering an area of 600 by 540 m.

Each of the grid squares was thoroughly searched for remains of stone constructions or surface indications of occupation. Forty-six structures were noted and sketched on an over-all site plan (fig. 1), about twice as many as Lothrop had originally mapped. Most of them are big, low platforms, which presumably had summit structures of wood and thatch. Three of these platforms had small, shrine-like temples on top. Besides platforms, low, dry, stone walls are common, although they are apparently not house-lot markers as at Mayapan (Bullard, 1952; 1954). They are described later in sections on architecture and settlement patterns. The platforms may have supported domiciliary structures; if so, they were of considerable size, and perhaps elite residences. Structure 39, for example, measures nearly 65 m long and 32 m wide. To the west of our mapped area are at least a dozen other, small unmapped platforms, and the site apparently ends about where the extended grid lines do. There are no unmapped structures to the north, east, or south of our gridded area. To the west there are a few scattered structures for a further distance of some 50 m; as this area is in pasture today, surface observation was greatly facilitated.

To test settlement pattern further, a technique that produced excellent results in the Chontalpa region in Tabasco was followed. There the problem was to determine whether a count of house mounds (in this case made of earth) alone would provide a total picture of the population distribution on a site, since it was perfectly possible that only a small fraction of the population erected platforms upon which to place houses. The solution consisted in digging small trenches at the junctions of grid lines to test the depth of organic soil deposition, density of ceramic remains, and presence of features such as hearths, burials, and house floors. At Tancah the trenches were all 1 by 1.5 m in surface area and wherever possible were excavated to bedrock.

Wherever grid lines crossed inside Group A or B, or on top of platforms, trenches were not excavated. Trenches falling near the edge or on the slope of platforms were moved down to the edges. Soil deposit in these excavations ranged from none at all at surface bedrock to 1.4 m in the midden area northeast of Group A, in general averaging 0.4 to 0.8 m. In all, 184 trenches were excavated, giving an excellent quantitative profile of the settlement pattern of the site. In addition to the data offered for settlement-pattern studies, excellent horizontal seriation was achieved, and the material filled out our knowledge of Tancah ceramics, as much of the pottery from the stratigraphic tests is in fragmentary condition.

Since most of the trenches yielded very small samples, those from the same north-south grid line, or part of the grid line, were grouped together for laboratory analysis and cataloguing, after total sherd counts by individual trench had been made. The north-south grid lines were selected for sherd grouping because the major axis of the site is east-west and the stratigraphic tests suggested strongly that sherd complexes would sort out along this axis as to phase. A number of trenches yielding abundant samples were studied separately and could be used as controls.

In addition to mapping and settlement-pattern trenching, sixteen stratigraphic tests were made in Groups A and B and at several other structures to establish the internal chronology of Tancah. Lothrop's (1924) analysis of the architecture indicated essential differences from that at Tulum. As the sites are only 2 km apart this diversity seemed to suggest that they were occupied at different chronological periods. Our excavations confirmed this possibility and also established a series of ceramic phases in the history of the site.

EXCAVATIONS

Group A Stratigraphic Trenches

The area within and immediately outside Group A proved to be the most productive at Tancah for stratigraphy. Only here were found a complex series of floor levels and deep refuse deposits. No trenches were excavated into structures, and no building stratigraphy was attempted. All the trenches were made along the edges of the base platforms of pyramids and temples, on their plaza side with only a few exceptions. The following trenches were excavated.

Trench 1

Trench 1 was a 1-m-wide excavation along the west or plaza side of Structure 1 (a high pyramid with a small east-coast shrine on top). It runs from the stairway south to the southwest corner of the pyramid. A series of plaza floors separated by fill were encountered, and a good stratigraphic sequence was obtained. Levels were defined as follows:

Level 1. Top soil level to 0.3 m; this level postdates the final phase of floor construction in the plaza, and the sherd assembly proved to be almost 100 per cent Tulum Buff Paste Censer ware. The lower limit is arbitrary.

Level 2. The lower part of the top soil zone running from 0.3 to 0.65 m. The soil in both Level 1 and Level 2 consists of a dry, powdery black humus. At 0.65 m the last floor in the history of plaza construction was uncovered; it defines the lower limit of the level. Here the base of the final or outer pyramid platform is well preserved—the only part of it that is.

Level 3. In this discussion floors will be numbered running from top to bottom; the floor just noted will be referred to as Floor 1. Level 3 refers to the fill between Floor 1, occurring at a depth of 0.65 m, and Floor 2, at 1.75 m. It consists of brown earth and small chunks of lime-stone. A small sherd sample was picked up in this level.

Floor 1 is poorly preserved, presumably owing to root action. Floor 2, on the other hand, is about 0.1 m thick, hard, compact, and in almost perfect condition.

Level 4. Below Floor 2 is a zone 0.35 m deep of small fragments of limestone mixed with brown earth followed by a succession of three masonry floors, all compressed into a band but 0.28 m thick. Floors 3 and 4 are in a very fragmentary state, but 5 is well defined and preserved. Between the floors occurs fill similar to that noted above.

Level 4 is defined as the space between Floors 2 and 5, or between 1.75 and 2.5 m below the present surface. One of the best sherd samples in the plaza came from this level.

Level 5. Below Floor 5 there is 0.85 m of loose, grainy, crumbly medium-brown earth with no stone at all. It almost surely represents an old soil level and predates all construction at Group A. It is well sealed off from Level 4 by Floor 5. From Level 5 a good ceramic sample was obtained, probably representing one of our earliest samples from the site. Along with pottery, fragments of human bone and shell beads were found. Below this soil layer, 3.35 m below the surface of the top soil, bedrock was reached.

Trench 2

A 1-m-wide trench excavated along the base of the stairway of Structure 8, a small temple on a high platform. This trench is not on the plaza side of the building. The following stratigraphic levels were defined:

Level 1. From 0 to 0.9 m. The lower limit of this level is defined by a well preserved masonry floor 0.1 m thick. This is Floor 2. The thinner, almost destroyed Floor 1 lies above at a depth of 0.35 to 0.4 m, but its condition precludes its use as a stratigraphic datum. Above the first floor occurs typical powdery black humus. Between Floors 1 and 2 is a fill of brown soil mixed with small limestone fragments. All sherds from above Floor 2 were lumped together in a single sample.

Level 2. Below Floor 2, to 1.6 m below the surface, is a thin layer of soil and small chunks of limestone which in turn rests on a bed of large fragments of dry limestone fill. The cap of earth and smaller fragments was evidently applied to level off the top of the bed preparatory to laying the masonry floor—a construction profile for floors that is typical of Tancah. All sherds from this construction unit were grouped together.

Level 3. Below the above-mentioned bed of large chunks of limestone down to bedrock. This level is composed of a loose, crumbly soil similar in texture and color to that of Level 5 in Trench 1, and here, as in Trench 1, it rests on bedrock. The maximum depth of Trench 2 was 1.9 m. All sherd samples from this trench are small.

Trench 3

A trench 1.5 m wide, 3 m long, running along the south edge of the platform in front of the doorway of Structure 10, a small temple on a low platform. The door of the temple faces outward from the plaza, and the trench is therefore not on the plaza side. Floor stratigraphy was simple. Two levels were defined.

Level 1. Top soil component, from 0 to 0.2 m. A small sample was collected from this level.

Level 2. Approximately 0.2 m below the surface are remains of a badly preserved floor. Below the floor is a single layer of flat limestone slabs, which in turn rests on a cap of small stones and brown earth 0.2 m thick. Finally, below this is a 0.9-m fill, consisting of large chunks of limestone, which rests on bedrock. Everything below the floor obviously represents a single constructional unit, and all sherds below it are grouped together as Level 2. The total depth of the trench is 1.4 m.

A good ceramic sample was obtained from this level. In the northwest corner of the trench a burial was uncovered lying on bedrock and against the platform face: an adult female in a flexed position with a large bowl inverted over the head and shoulders. The burial evidently took place before any construction was raised, the large chunks of limestone at the base of the construction unit having been thrown on top of the vessel, crushing it. Most of the vessel was recoverable and restorable (fig. 15,1).

Also excavated was a complete, small, tripod cuplike censer of Tulum Buff Paste Censer ware (very similar to vessels from Mayapan), at the level of Floor 1 (figs. 8,b,30; 15,h).

Trench 4

Trench 4 is 1 m wide, running along the edge of the platform of Structure 6 from the stairway to the south corner. It is in the plaza, and floor stratigraphy is very complex. The trench was not excavated to bedrock because of danger of cave-in. Structure 6 is a large (for the east coast) temple set on a terraced but only moderately high pyramid.

Level 1. Top soil layer, 0.4 m in depth. The lower limit is coincident with Floor 1, a badly preserved masonry floor. A small sherd sample came from this level.

Level 2. A constructional unit consisting of 0.5 m of fill between Floor 1 and a postulated Floor 2. It has a typical profile of a thin top layer of earth with small fragments of limestone and a thicker bottom layer of large chunks of limestone. A good sherd sample was picked up from this level.

Level 3. If a masonry floor existed below Level 2, it has been entirely destroyed. There is, however, a distinct construction unit, a duplication of the profile found in Level 2, with the small-stone-and-earth cap lying directly below the big-stone layer of Level 2. Level 3 runs from 0.9 to 1.8 m depth. A small ceramic sample was collected from it.

Below Level 3 the top cap of earth-and-small-stone fill of a lower construction unit could be observed, but excavation was halted as explained above. Here again no traces of a masonry floor separated the levels.

Trench 5

Trench 5 was a clearing operation, not a true trench. Roof and wall debris were cleared off the floor of part of Structure 10 to get a ceramic sample from the surface of the floor. Only a few sherds were recovered. An altar was uncovered against the back wall of the inner room.

Trench 6

Trench 6 was another plaza trench, situated along Structure 3, with a complex series of floors. Unfortunately only small sherd samples were collected.

Level 1. Top soil layer, 0.8 m deep. A small sample was found in this level.

Level 2. Below the top soil is a succession of four floors. Floors 1 and 2 and Floors 2 and 3 are separated by 0.15 m of earth and small-stone fill, but Floor 3 rests directly on Floor 4. The floors are very thin and poorly preserved. The total depth between the top of Floor 1 and Floor 4 is but 0.5 m. All sherds between Floors 1 and 4 were grouped into a single sample.

Level 3. Between Floors 4 and 5, or between 1.2 and 1.7 m below the surface. Below Floor 4 is a fill made of large, dry-laid chunks of limestone.

Level 4. From below Floor 5 to bedrock, from 1.7 to 2.4 m below the surface. This level consists of a fill of small stones and brown earth. At approximately 2 m are a few remains of a sixth floor.

Group B   Stratigraphic Trenches

In this group excavations were concentrated on Structures 12 and 17. Structure 12, a large temple on a high terraced pyramid base, is one of the most beautifully preserved buildings at Tancah; Structure 17 is a mound of rubble with only traces of standing walls.

Trench 7

In initiating excavations in Structure 17 a trench was first dug paralleling the plaza side of the base of the mound to locate the final plaza floor. This trench, 0.5 m wide by 4.5 m long and centered on the mound, was dug to a well preserved plaza floor. A small ceramic sample was collected in it.

Trench 8

Trench 8 actually was a clearing rather than an excavation. The loose rubble of the almost destroyed outer Structure 17 was removed from the slope of the mound in a band 4.5 m wide (the length of Trench 7) extending from Trench 7 to the temple on top. The clearing of rubble revealed an interesting series of architectural details which is summarized in the drawings (fig. 3,a). The remains of the stairways presumably are all that is left of the outer building within the trench area. The preserved walls back of the stairway are undoubtedly remains of an inner pyramid that evidently consisted of at least three terraces, the top two of which were round. The third, with a rectangular base, was partly destroyed by the Maya when they built the outer and final temple. A small sample was collected from the rubble, but no attempt was made to excavate into the inner structure. The rubble was thrown back into the trench to preserve the inner building.

The wall base is all that is left of the temple on top. It apparently dates with the outer structure.

Trench 9

A trench 4 m long by 2.5 m wide was excavated from the stairway of Structure 12 extending north to the northeast corner of the basal terrace. It is on the plaza side of the building. The following levels were defined.

Level 1. Top soil component, 0.6 m deep, overlying a well preserved masonry floor. A large sherd sample was collected.

Level 2. Below the masonry floor, which is about 0.5 m thick, and extending down to bedrock. The level, composed of earth and small-stone fill, is about 0.5 m deep. The total depth of the trench here was but 1.1 m, in striking contrast to those excavated in Group A. A small sherd sample was collected from this level. A complete knife of white chert was also found (fig. 19,a,1).

Trench 10

Trench 10 was excavated along the back of Structure 12, running south from the northwest corner for 2 m; it was 1.5 m wide. A small sherd sample was collected. No constructional or arbitrary levels were defined.

Miscellaneous Stratigraphic Trenches

Trench 11

One of the settlement-pattern trenches (SP 29), about 20 m northeast of Group A, proved to run through the richest midden or occupation refuse deposit on the site. Some 1.4 m of rich, black, powdery humus overlying the bedrock at this point yielded the heaviest sherd sample from Tancah. Over 1000 sherds were collected from this trench with a surface area but 1 by 1.5 m. The material was taken out in two arbitrary levels: Level 1, 0 to 0.75 m; Level 2, 0.75 to 1.4 m. To augment the stratigraphic value of the sample, Trench 11 was excavated adjoining SP Trench 29, leaving a 0.15-m unexcavated wall between the two. The trench, measuring 3 m north-south by 2 m east-west, was excavated by arbitrary 0.3-m levels. The following levels were defined:

Level 1	0-0.3 m	51 sherds
Level 2	0.3-0.6 m	131 sherds
Level 3	0.6-0.9 m	154 sherds
Level 4	0.9-1.3 m	391 sherds

In the northeast corner of the trench, in Level 2, parts of a human skeleton appeared along with an almost complete pottery vessel (fig. 15,k). A 1-m-square extension was dug north of this corner to excavate the burial, but no further traces of the skeleton were found. A heavy concentration of sherds was picked up in this extension. Finally, the earth wall between SP Trench 29 and Trench 11 was removed and the sherds were collected.

Trench 12

Trench 12, 1 m wide and 2.5 m long, was excavated to bedrock (a depth of 2.2 m) along a low terrace at the front, north side, of Structure 50, down through Structure 51, the big platform on which the terrace rests. The following levels were defined.

Level 1. From the present surface of the platform to the first definable masonry floor. Although there undoubtedly was a floor on top of the platform, no traces of it remain. Floor 1, situated at a depth of 0.7 m below the present platform surface, is a well preserved, hard, 0.1-m-thick floor, presumably representing the surface of an older, smaller platform. The 0.7 m of fill above it is mainly earth and medium-sized chunks of limestone. A small ceramic sample came from this level.

Level 2. Below Floor 1 is a 0.1-m cap of small fragments of limestone and earth. Below this occurred a 0.15-m-thick layer of brown earth which in turn rested on 0.45 m of large limestone fragments. From Floor 1 to the base of the last layer is defined as Level 2. The sherd sample from this level was very large.

Level 3. Below Level 2 is 0.7 m of fill, mostly earth mixed with small stone fragments. A good sherd sample was collected in this level which showed important differences in ware frequencies from the sample in Level 2.

Trench 13

Three meters long by 1.2 m wide, running along the south edge of the south stairway to Structure 51 (platform under Structure 50). The trench was excavated through 1 m of black top soil heavily saturated with sherds and was carried down to bedrock. No arbitrary levels were kept. A very rich sample of pottery was picked up from this trench.

Trench 14

A 3.0 by 1.2 m trench excavated along the west side of Structure 42. No arbitrary levels were defined here; the soil cover, black humus mixed with sherds, was approximately 0.8 m deep.

Trench 15

This trench ran along the west edge of Structure 55 from the stairway to the southwest corner. It measured 1.2 by 2.8 m, and the depth varied from 1.5 to 2.0 m. Approximately 0.8 m below the surface were found remains of a badly preserved floor. All sherds from above this depth were separated as Level 1; all below, as Level 2.

A number of features were uncovered in the course of this excavation (fig. 3,f). First a column drum, 0.2 m thick and 0.3 m in diameter, with its base penetrating below the floor, was discovered near the stairway side of the trench. Next, an uncarved stela was found lying on its side 0.4 m below the present soil level and 0.3 m above the floor. Below it were fragments of several human skeletons, but as the floor is completely destroyed in this area their relative position is uncertain; some appear to have been 0.5 to 0.1 m above the floor, others just below it. Possibly they represent intrusive burials, the floor having been destroyed at the time of the burial. Finally, a stone wall was discovered running diagonally across the trench, probably the face of an old platform of which the masonry floor was the top. Evidently a low platform was constructed first, and the stone column and stela probably go with it. Later the small pyramid, Structure 55, was erected over part of it, and the floor of the old platform was broken through for the burial. The earlier platform rests on bedrock.

Trench 16

Trench 16, 1.7 by 3.2 m, was excavated from the stairway to the southeast corner of the platform of the Rancho Temple (fig. 3, d). The soil cover was only 0.3 to 0.4 m deep here, and only a small sherd sample was picked up.

CERAMIC CHRONOLOGY AT TANCAH

Introduction

The ceramic chronology at Tancah seems clear. When the samples are combined with those from near-by Tulum we have an almost continuous ceramic record of northern Quintana Roo from Late Formative to the Conquest period. On the basis of the 16 stratigraphic trenches (chart 1), and the settlement-pattern trench data (chart 2), the following observations and conclusions can be noted.

The Tulum ceramic complex is found in some abundance at Tancah (Tulum Red, Tulum Plain, Tulum Buff Paste Censer, V Fine Orange, Mayapan Black-on-cream), especially censer ware. Heavy samples always occur in and around ceremonial structures, the wares generally being restricted to top soil samples from above the first preserved plaza floor or platform. In the areas around the ceremonial structures very few sherds occur. The conclusion seems inescapable that the Tulum Period occupation of the site follows the pattern, found on many Meso-american sites, of ceremonial reuse—probably of ruined and abandoned buildings—with no settlement occupation to go with it. Some building activities were carried on, and some shrines, as at Structure 1, were certainly built during the Tulum Period (the original temple being destroyed and some of the stones reused for the newer, smaller construction). Lothrop (1924, p. 121) noted the incongruity of the small shrines situated on large pyramidal bases; I think the explanation lies in this ceremonial rebuilding and reuse during the Tulum Period. The same situation was discovered at Coba (Thompson, Pollock, Charlot, 1932, pp. 34, 112). Structure 12 in Group B with its large, imposing temple on a high, steep pyramidal base is probably a good example of the original Classic architecture of Tancah. Besides building, a considerable amount of repair work must have accompanied this reuse.

To judge from the concentrations of censer ware on top of the final floor around Groups A and B, these buildings must have been rather heavily utilized.

Of great interest is the abrupt shift from earlier to Tulum Period wares (chart 1). Wherever floor levels are well preserved the ceramics show a complete change, indicating the arrival of, or use of the structures by, a foreign group without antecedents in the Tancah area. A close parallel is seen with the introduction of Toltec architecture at Chichen Itza.

Group A

The samples from Group A, along with Trench 11, a few meters northeast of the group, represent the deepest stratigraphic sequence from the site. The picture is consistent in spite of the

CHART I FREQUENCIES OF WARES FROM STRATIGRAPHIC TRENCHES AT TANCAH

GROUP A — WARES OR TYPES

Boxed numbers = sherd count. Percentage scale = width of box (0 10 ... 50 ... 100).

Trench	Level	Total	Unclassified	Regional Polychrome	Tancah Striated	Tancah Plain	Tancah Variegated	Tancah Red	Tulum Buff Paste Censer	Tulum Plain	Tulum Red
Trench 1	Level 1	93							87		5
Trench 1	Level 2	21	2	7	8	2	1				
Trench 1	Level 3	18			10	3	4				
Trench 1	Level 4	95			17	31	29	18			
Trench 1	Level 5	128			22	32	18	56			
Trench 2	Level 1	58			7	7	3	4	37		
Trench 2	Level 2	100			22	28	25	25			
Trench 2	Level 3	27			5	5	4	13			
Trench 3	Level 1	7							1		6
Trench 3	Level 2	89		2	12	29	28	18			
Trench 4	Level 1	65		4	4				45		
Trench 4	Level 2	207	4		31	67	52	53			
Trench 4	Level 3	34			5	8	5	16			
Trench 6	Level 1	35							33		2
Trench 6	Level 2	26			6	7	4	1	8		
Trench 6	Level 3	32			15	2	9	6			
Trench 6	Level 4	59			25		21	13			

GROUP B — WARES OR TYPES (MISCELLANEOUS)

Trench	Level	Total	Unclassified	Yucatan Slate and Thin Slate	Regional Polychrome	Tancah Restricted Orifice	Tancah Striated	Tancah Plain	Tancah Variegated	Tancah Red	Vista Alegre Striated	Tulum Buff Paste Censer	Mayapan Black-on-Cream	V Fine Orange	Tulum Plain	Tulum Red
TR.7		26		3								22				—
TR.8		19		12				5								2
TR.9	Level 1	67		5								61				
TR.9	Level 2	55		2	3		13	26		8						4
Trench 11	Level 1	182			3		21	43	59	56						
Trench 11	Level 2	164					27	27	63	47						
Trench 11	Level 3	391					104	5	75	207						
Trench 12	Level 1	26				1	1				3	9	1	2	5	2
Trench 12	Level 2	93		19	7		47	4	5	11						
Trench 12	Level 3	40		8	19	1	20	6	1	3						
TR.13		272	26	107	28	2	62	9		11					20	2
TR.14		95	1	10	14	2	23	21	12	4		8	5			
TR.15	Level 1	40		8						6		26				
TR.15	Level 2	177	9	53	27		65	8		10						
TR.16		42		1				1				40				

generally small samples. The clearest relationship occurs between Tancah Red and Tancah Variegated (chart 1). In our samples Tancah Red dominates in the bottom levels and shows a history of gradually decreasing importance. Tancah Variegated, on the other hand, increases to a peak in the middle of the sequences and declines sharply afterward or steadily decreases in frequency. At the base levels of our best trenches (1, 2, 4, 11) Tancah Red runs between 42 and 53 per cent of all wares, dropping to about one-half this frequency in the following levels and finally below 10 per cent in the upper levels of Trenches 1, 2, and 4. Variegated runs generally between 14 and 20 per cent in the lowest levels, increases to 25-41 per cent in the next level up, and drops sharply below 10 per cent in the upper levels of the Group A trenches. Trench 11 evidently lacks the final phase of the history of these wares and yields frequencies equivalent to those in the lower and middle levels of Group A trenches.

Regional Polychrome has a limited distribution in these trenches, falling always in the final constructional level in the plaza trenches proper and in the uppermost level of Trench 11. It evidently coincides with the decline of both Tancah Red and Variegated simultaneously. The samples include mostly Tzakol shapes (basal flange bowls dominating). The ware is minor, running around 2 per cent consistently except in Trench 1, where it rises to one-third of the total sherd sample (a small sample of only 19 sherds). Of great significance in the Group A samples, as well as Trench 11, is the complete lack of any Yucatan Medium Slate or Thin Slate. Moreover, only two sherds of these wares appeared in any settlement-pattern trenches along Grid Lines 1 through 10, which cover the eastern half of the surveyed part of the site. I suspect that the plaza was completely abandoned when slate wares were introduced at Tancah, although this conclusion is perhaps premature before building stratigraphy is attempted. No restricted orifice bowls, striated or plain, occur in these trenches either, another strong argument that the plaza was abandoned before Yucatan Slate ware was introduced.

The unslipped plain and striated ware sequence is not clear. Some trenches show a definite trend from striated to plain ware, but in others the seriation is reversed. Interpretation is complicated by the fact that striation does not always occur over the entire vessel, and the only difference between striated and plain wares lies in the striations. Combining the two wares, Tancah Striated and Tancah Plain, we find in all the trenches a gradual increase in frequency as compared with slipped wares from the earliest to the latest levels (in this picture all top levels are excluded, since these are post-Classic samples; therefore in all trenches Tancah Plain and Striated drop off sharply in Level 1).

In summary, then, our Group A excavations indicate the following stratigraphic picture: (1) A continuous long period of construction with three well defined ceramic phases: an early, in which Tancah Red dominates over Tancah Variegated, and slipped wares over unslipped; a middle, in which Tancah Variegated dominates over Tancah Red and in which unslipped wares increase in importance, running in general 50 per cent of the samples; and a final late phase marked by increased percentages of unslipped wares, decline of both Tancah Variegated and Red, and the sudden appearance of Regional Polychrome. (2) A cessation in use and occupation of Group A. (3) Reuse and slight building projects in which the Tulum ceramic complex completely replaces all Classic wares and is unrelated to them.

Group B

The situation in Group B is entirely different (chart 1). No deep stratigraphy occurs there, and the plaza may even have been left unpaved. At most, it was paved but once or twice in the history of its construction. The soil deposit runs generally less than 1 m.

Trench 9 was excavated in two arbitrary levels. Level 1 contained 91 per cent Tulum Buff Paste Censer ware, 6 per cent Tulum Red, and the remainder Yucatan Slate ware, which we noted as absent at Group A. Level 2 yielded entirely Classic Period wares, in the following percentages: Tancah Red, 15; Tancah Striated, 24; Tancah Plain, 47 (continuing the trend of unslipped wares noted for Group A); Regional Polychrome, 5; Yucatan Slate, 9. Trench 10, a shallow trench with no arbitrary levels, shows the same combination of Classic wares—Tancah Plain, Regional Polychrome, Yucatan Slate (here running to 25 per cent)—with a typically heavy showing of Tulum Buff Paste Censer. Trench 7, another shallow excavation on the plaza side of Structure 17 (fig. 3,a), yielded mostly Tulum wares but with a secondary concentration of Yucatan Slate (11 per cent). Trench 8 was dug into Structure 17 and includes sherds from the rubble of the outer structure. Here Classic Period wares comprised 89 per cent of the sample, with Yucatan Slate running to 63 per cent.

The data suggest that we have a reuse of the plaza during the Tulum Period and that most of the construction dates from the period correlated with the appearance of Yucatan Slate, which we noted as completely absent in our Group A samples.

One of the major chronological problems at Tancah is the relation between the Group A and Group B sherd complexes. In spite of the small samples, the divergences, being consistent, are statistically significant. Of great importance is the complete lack of Tancah Variegated in the Group B samples.

The two trenches excavated in and around Structure 51 give the clearest-cut vertical relationships between these two complexes of wares. Trench 12, dug into the structure and running along the north side of the surmounting shrine (Structure 50; fig. 3,b), yielded three constructional levels. In the upper level, in the top soil deposit on top of the platform, is the same sherd assemblage noted in the Group B collections, with Tulum wares running 65 per cent and Yucatan Slate ware 31 per cent. Level 2 is a pure Classic sample with Tancah Striated, Yucatan Slate, and Regional Polychrome all in heavy percentages. Of 93 sherds classified from this level, only 1 is Tancah Variegated, as opposed to 19 sherds of Yucatan Slate, again showing the antithetical relationship between these two wares. Level 3, on the other hand, which may be a preconstructional level (small fragments of limestone scattered through mainly brown earth), repeats the sherd assemblages from Group A with the exception of a heavy showing of Regional Polychrome. The results of this trench suggest strongly that Yucatan Slate ware came into Tancah toward the end of the occupation and use of Group A.

Trench 13, dug along the outside of Structure 51, penetrated a shallow but rich sherd deposit with no levels, arbitrary or otherwise. Practically all wares found on the east coast of Yucatan were picked up in this excavation, although Tancah Variegated, significantly enough, is not present, and Tancah Red amounts to only 4 per cent. The bulk of the sample is striated jars, among which are rims of both Tancah Striated and Vista Alegre Striated, and Yucatan Slate. Our best samples of slate wares came from this trench. In addition to the wares mentioned, small percentages of Tancah Plain, Regional Polychrome, Tulum wares, Polished Black, and possibly Puuc Red ware and Calderitas Polychrome were present.

Trench 15, dug along the front (west wide) of Structure 55, presented two construction levels, one above and one below a masonry floor (fig. 3,f). The floor was badly destroyed, however, and some mixing of samples undoubtedly occurred. Level 1 is mainly Tulum Buff Paste Censer with a strong representation of Yucatan Slate and Tancah Red wares. Some of the last may actually have been Tulum Red; all were tiny body sherds, and identification was not certain for some of them. Level 2, on the other hand, is mostly Tancah and/or Vista Alegre Striated (no definite rims of the latter) and Yucatan Slate. Regional Polychrome appears in appreciable amount (15 per cent).

CHART 2. FREQUENCIES OF WARES FROM SETTLEMENT PATTERN TRENCHES AT TANCAH

WARES OR TYPES. BOXED NUMBERS = SHERD COUNT. PERCENTAGE SCALE = WIDTH OF BOX (scale 0 · 10 · 50 · 100).

Upper section

Grid Line Nos.	Settlement Pattern Trench Nos.	Tulum Red	Tulum Plain	V Fine Orange	Mayapan Black-on-Cream	Vista Alegre Striated	Tancah Red	Tancah Variegated	Tancah Plain	Tancah Striated	Regional Polychrome	Yucatan Slate and Thin Slate	Total
22	170-171	1	3		4		10		17	17	11	28	91
23	172-174		17	1			5		20	8	3	42	96
24, 25, 26	175-182						5		15	10		27	57

Selected trenches with heavy sherd yields

Grid Line Nos.	Settlement Pattern Trench Nos.	Tulum Red	Tulum Plain	Mayapan Black-on-Cream	Vista Alegre Striated	Tancah Red	Tancah Variegated	Tancah Plain	Tancah Striated	Regional Polychrome	Yucatan Slate and Thin Slate	Total
2	11					37	15	17	41			110
3	29 Level 1					131	60	40	82			313
3	29 Level 2					105	46	36	93			280
3	30, 31					86	36	50	17	2		191
4	33					42	9	19	29			99
4	34					17	30	22	12	1		82
4	47					80	23	34	26			163
6	48					32	27	35	23			117
6	49-50					54	5	31	75			175
6	53					35	21	28	23			107
7	61					24	13	18	26			81
13	134 Level 1	14	2	4	2	1		4			13	40
13	134 Level 2					16		17	29	10	28	100

Lower section

Grid Line Nos.	Settlement Pattern Trench Nos.	Tulum Red	Tulum Plain	Tulum Buff Paste Censer	Vista Alegre Striated	Tancah Red	Tancah Variegated	Tancah Plain	Tancah Striated	Tancah Restricted Orifice	Regional Polychrome	Yucatan Slate and Thin Slate	Total
1	1-8		14			21	3	43	12		1		93
2	9-22 (minus 11)	1				18	9	18	12		1		58
3	23-28					45	39	56	9				161
4	32, 35-39	2				43	12	19	15				89
5	40-46	1				63	17	34	33				149
6	51-59 (minus 53)	1	5			77	33	45	41				197
7	60-71 (minus 61)		4			77	38	54	37	3			211
8	72-84		2			48	43	60	30	2			183
9	85-95		3			32	4	48	20		1	1	98
10	96-107		6			27	23	53	4		5	14	141
11	108-116					16	10	28	13		3		73
12	117-128		8			5		40	12		5	52	124
13	131-136 (minus 134)	1	20	1		18		17	7			31	90
14	137-140		2			12		25	5		12	34	103
14	141-144				1	8		7			5	11	31
15	145-147	1				21		12	39			36	134
15	148-152	1	17			15		9	21		3	51	120
16-21						7		15				7	32

173

Trench 14, a shallow but productive trench dug along the west base of Structure 42, did not produce a definitive sample. All important wares occurring at Tancah are present, and no association or complex of wares dominates the sample.

Settlement-Pattern Trenches

The sharp dichotomy in ceramics between Group A and Group B is borne out by the distribution of wares in the settlement-pattern trenches (chart 2).

The 107 trenches dug along settlement-pattern Grid Lines 1 to 10 (fig. 1) produced a total of 1 Yucatan Slate and 6 Regional Polychrome sherds. The rest of the sample conforms to the frequencies analyzed for the Early and Middle Phases of Group A, with the following over-all ware percentages:

	Range, %	Mode
Tancah Red	19-48	30-40
Tancah Variegated	3-24	13-18
Tancah Striated	12-37	17-20
Tancah Plain	12-61	23-31
Tulum wares	1-15	3- 9

Yucatan Slate first appears in quantity in the Grid Line 11 trenches, and the samples contain a few sherds of Tancah Variegated. Grid Lines 12 to 26, or SP Trenches 117 to 182, did not yield a single sherd of Tancah Variegated, and Tancah Red never runs over 26 per cent of the samples, generally falling between 12 and 20 per cent. Tancah Plain and Tancah Striated continue in about the same frequency as before. The major new addition is Yucatan Slate ware, which ranges from 27 to 42 per cent of the samples. Regional Polychrome also increases, running between 2 and 12 per cent where it occurs and being completely lacking in samples from only three of the grid lines.

Tulum wares have about the same frequencies as around the eastern half of the site.

3. TULUM — EXCAVATIONS AND CERAMIC ANALYSIS

GENERAL DESCRIPTION

Tulum is the largest post-Classic site visited during the two field seasons, and along with Kantunil Kin and Tancah is one of the largest sites of any period in Quintana Roo. The only larger site reported is Coba. Lothrop (1924) has left a detailed, careful survey of the plan and architecture of Tulum, to which our field work contributed only minor additions or corrections. As the central and northern thirds of the site today are clean of vegetation, observation on the basis of surface surveys was possible. A brief description of the site plan (fig. 2) will help to orient the reader.

Tulum is situated on a rocky headland overlooking the sea. The seaward side of the site, except for one small stretch that is a natural opening or break in the sea cliff where the terrain drops down to a sandy beach (fig. 13,a), is naturally defended by high, steep limestone cliffs. The other three sides, north, west, and south, are surrounded by a dry stone wall.

In a survey of settlement patterns the site might be described in three sections. First is the area enclosed by the Great Wall, which includes all but two of the religious and civic buildings. It is a rectangular area, measuring 400 m north-south by 170 m east-west, or approximately 7 hectares (18 acres). The second unit is a smaller walled enclosure to the south, adjacent to the Main Enclosure. Roughly triangular, it has an area of approximately 5 hectares, or 12 acres. The total walled area is, then, approximately 12 hectares. The third unit is the space outside the walled enclosures. To the west the site and terrain slope off into low swamp, where no cultural material occurs. To the north on the rocky clifflike ridge paralleling the beach are two temples, approximately 400 and 600 m, respectively, from the north wall. South of the Lesser Enclosure is rocky ridge, and this is crisscrossed by a complex and extensive system of fortified double walls which must have a total length at least as great as the two site enclosures together. The walls, of low, dry stone, might better be called breastworks. The inhabitants of Tulum evidently had powerful enemies to the south.

The Main Enclosure, then, includes the most important structures and was the center of Tulum life. The area has a valley-like profile. A depression runs down the center from north to south, from which the terrain slopes upward to both the east and the west. The east summit terminates in sea cliff; the west, in a rocky ridge upon which is built the West Wall, the terrain then sloping off sharply to the swamp. Running from north to south, along the bottom of the trough, is a long, narrow avenue which is the architectonic axis of the site (fig. 2). Lothrop called it Main Street—a very apt label (fig. 13,b). A main avenue as an axis of site orientation is rare in the Maya area but common in the Mexican Meseta Central, being found at Xochicalco, Teotihuacan, and finally Tenochtitlan; it reflects the Mexican origin of much of post-Classic Yucatecan culture. Main Street was evidently not paved, but the edge was marked by a low wall varying in height from 0.3 to 1 m according to the size of the structure fronting it. It is lined by house platforms, or terraces and civic buildings, mainly palaces or residential structures, which lie along the northern two-thirds of the street. About halfway down the length of Main Street and 40 m east of it is the main religious complex of the site, a small plaza surrounded by masonry structures of which the Castillo, fronting on the east side of the plaza with its back to the sea cliff, is the most impressive in size.

In addition to the structures in the Main Plaza (Lothrop's Inner Enclosure) and along Main Street, there are a few isolated temples (Structures 45, 54, and 35) on two rocky knolls and over a cenote.

175

Just north of the Inner Enclosure, at a break in the sea cliff, the land drops down to a sandy beach and fans out into a flat low area that merges into the trough of Main Street, thus providing easy access to the otherwise well fortified site. It is tempting to think of the beach as a canoe port, and the expanded level space inland from it as the market place.

For settlement-pattern studies and excavations the site may be divided into a number of zones, as follows (fig. 2).

1. The Northwest Quadrant, the area between Main Street and the West Wall north of Structure 20. No public buildings occur in this zone; the terrain slopes gradually up from Main Street (figs. 3,g; 13,d). The only masonry structures are the individual front walls of the various house platforms that line Main Street. This area, in scrub bush at the time of my visit, was completely cleared, and surface examination revealed an abundance of occupational debris, sherds, and obsidian.

2. The Northeast Quadrant, the space east of Main Street and north of the Inner Enclosure. It includes the Cenote House (Structure 35) and Structure 54, both temples, and our postulated "Market" and "Port." As only one house platform occurs here, the area was probably little used as a habitation center, although the low level place called a "Market" has the deepest and heaviest refuse deposits on the site.

3. The Central Area, the middle of the site, including the area on both sides of Main Street (fig. 2). East of Main Street it was strictly a civic zone, being occupied by the Structures 21-25 Group (Palaces), Fresco Temple, and the Inner Enclosure. West of Main Street and fronting on it is Structure 20, another palace, and west of that a narrow, fairly level space showing some signs of occupation.

4. The Southern Area, the southern part of the site on both sides of Main Street. This area is heavily wooded so that surface observation was less effective. West of Main Street the terrain slopes very gradually up to the West Wall, about 50 m away. Signs of occupation west of Main Street are rather scanty, and no civic buildings occur. East of Main Street the terrain has a steep slope up to the sea cliff and had been reworked into a series of three or four terraces, only traces of which survive (fig. 3,g). The terraces were undoubtedly built as living spaces, and this part of the site was probably one of the main living areas of the ancient community. One civic building, Structure 54, a small temple, is on top of the ridge overlooking the sea.

Surprisingly, the enclosure south of the Main Enclosure shows little sign of use as either a civic or a habitation zone. Along the sea-cliff ridge in the vicinity of the south wall of the Main Enclosure are a few house terraces and fairly abundant signs of occupation, but most of the enclosed space lacked either soil or surface pottery.

Outside the immediate vicinity of the Great Wall evidence of house platforms or of occupation is very scanty. I found no justification for Lothrop's statement that Tulum and Tancah form almost a continuous settlement with scattered house platforms running from one site to the other. On the contrary, the settlement area at Tulum is sharply defined by the Great Wall. As we have seen, the same can be said of Tancah (although no wall is present); the two sites are separated by 2 km of bush and rocky terrain with only an occasional structure between.

Settlement-pattern excavations and survey were concentrated, then, on the area within the Main Enclosure. As at Tancah, grid lines were laid off at regular intervals, oriented on Main Street, which provided a useful base line (Grid Line 5).

In the Northwest Quadrant four grid lines were laid off running from Main Street to the West Wall, and along them small trenches of the type described for Tancah were excavated every 10 m, a total of 24 trenches (see fig. 2 and table 4). In the Southern Area five grid lines were laid off from east to west crossing the site at intervals of 40 m, and 53 trenches were excavated in this area, bringing the total of settlement-pattern trenches to 77. To obtain ceramic stratigraphy, 50 other trenches were excavated at Tulum, mainly along the edges of building platforms. These excavations are summarized in detail in the following section. In spite of the short season (about 4 weeks with a 6-man crew) the site was thoroughly tested, and we undoubtedly have a complete ceramic record.

EXCAVATIONS

Structure 47

Structure 47, probably a house platform, faces Main Street, being situated on the north side and just east of the Inner Enclosure. The ground slopes up sharply here, and the street side of the platform is approximately 1 m high but the upper edge merges directly into the sloping terrain. The platform is faced with roughly tooled stone blocks, has a fill of broken chunks of limestone, and probably supported a pole-and-thatch structure.

Three trenches were excavated in and around Structure 47.

Trench 1. One meter wide, running along the west edge (street side) of the platform from the stairway to the southwest corner, and approximately 4 m long. Only 0.1 m of soil overlies the bedrock here, and a small sherd sample was collected.

Trench 2. One meter by 5.5 m along the south side of the platform from the southwest corner up the slope. Over-all soil depth here was generally 0.1 m with small pockets as deep as 0.3 m. A fair-sized sample was collected.

Trench 3. This trench, 1.5 m wide, was dug into the platform fill at right angles to Trench 2. The fill, besides dry limestone fragments, contains black soil and abundant cultural debris in the form of human and animal bones, sherds, obsidian blades and cores, snail shell, and grinding stones (manos and metates). In all probability the ancient inhabitants of Tulum scooped up this cultural refuse from dumps along Main Street and used it as fill. On top of the platform is a thin layer of black organic soil, presumably post-construction debris, with a small concentration of sherds, and below that is platform fill, with no preserved masonry floor. Most of the sherds were from the fill. The trench was excavated down to bedrock. The only inner structures encountered were the burial platforms described below.

Construction 1 was evidently a burial platform situated on bedrock and about in the center of the structure. It was of masonry, about 0.25 m high, with a plaster facing and a fill of small stones. Rectangular in plan, it measured 0.9 by 1.2 m.

Construction 2 is another burial platform, also resting on bedrock, just west of Construction 1. In height and width it is similar to Construction 1, but the length, which was not determined, is at least twice as great.

On each construction was discovered a mass of very badly preserved human bones, representing several children. No offerings occurred. The possibility seems strong that the bones were those of victims sacrificed as a preliminary act to the construction of the house platform.

Structures 21-25 Group

Two large palaces situated on the north edge of Main Street are connected by a broad, low terrace. Since Lothrop's visit, the Instituto Nacional de Antropología e Historia has made a number of trenches in the group to reveal architectural details. Lothrop's (1924, pl. 25) plan shows simply a low, broad terrace between the two palaces which fronts on Main Street where it has an elevation of about 0.5 m and merges eastward with the rising terrain. The Instituto explorations disclosed that there was once a sunken court where this connecting terrace is and that the original group included Structure 21 and a low platform to the east. Later on the court was filled and the terrace was constructed, covering the stairway of the east platform. On the north end of this new terrace Structure 25 was erected, and the group was completed in its present form. This sequence is suggested by the following facts:

1. The terrace is clearly an extension of Structure 21, and does not run under it.
2. An Instituto trench dug along the east edge of the terrace revealed the buried terrace face and stairway of the east platform.
3. The terrace runs underneath Structure 25, and the stairway of Structure 25 does not run below the terrace fill.

Our plan of the site (fig. 2) clarifies these relationships. We have, then, a complex group with various building stages, most of which our trenches cover.

Nine excavations (Trenches 4-12) were made in the group; they are summarized below.

Trench 4. One meter wide along the west edge of the connecting terrace in what is Main Street, and running south from the stairway for 3 m. Soil here was rather deep, in general about 0.5 to 0.6 m with occasional pockets nearly 1 m. A good ceramic sample was collected in two arbitrary levels.

Trench 5. A 1-m-wide trench running along the south side of Structure 25 on top of the connecting terrace from the stairway east for 2.5 m. It was excavated through the terrace fill to bedrock. The trench profile shows 0.2 to 0.3 m of black top soil separated from the terrace fill by a masonry floor. The fill is typical limestone fragments mixed with soil but almost without cultural refuse. The top soil, on the other hand, yielded a heavy sherd sample with several restorable vessels. One of them was an almost complete effigy vessel, evidently used as a censer, which was found at the angle between stairway and the palace platform on top of the masonry floor (fig. 15,d). This floor is 1.42 m below the top of the platform of Structure 25.

Trench 6. Along the same side of Structure 25 from the stairway west to the southwest corner of the structure platform. It was dug only to the masonry floor, which on this side of the stairway was well preserved. A very heavy sherd sample was picked up, including several reconstructable vessels. Again, an effigy vessel was recovered at the inner angle formed by the stairway with the platform; evidently one was placed on each side of the stairway (fig. 15,i). This one is of different form from the first.

Trench 7. A 1-m-wide trench dug along the base of the stairway of Structure 25. The masonry floor, which evidently covers the entire terrace between the two palaces, was again encountered. It was broken through in order to find out whether the stairway of the palace continued down into the terrace fill; since it did not, Structure 25 is dated as post-terrace construction. Only a few sherds were scattered through this trench.

Trench 8. A 1 by 2 m trench excavated into the fill of the buried platform that bordered the sunken court on the east. It is 1 m or so back of the platform face and just southeast of the stair-way. Presumably the pottery sample from this fill should predate our above-floor refuse deposits from Trenches 5 and 6. The trench was dug to bedrock. Sherds were abundant in the fill and sparse in the top soil above it.

Trench 9. A 1.2-m-wide trench dug from the stairway to the southeast corner along the south edge of Structure 21. The soil here is only 0.2 to 0.3 m deep, but a heavy sample of pottery was collected, mainly censer ware. No floors were encountered.

Trench 10. A 1.2-m-wide trench excavated from the stairway of Structure 21 westward to the angle formed between the main part of the building and the south wing. A very heavy sherd sample was uncovered here, mainly household wares, including several reconstructable vessels of Tulum Red ware. Soil again was only 0.2 to 0.3 m deep, and no levels were defined.

Trench 11. One of the deepest and richest trenches dug at Tulum. It runs along the base of the back (north) stairway of Structure 25 and is about 1.4 m deep. The samples were taken out in 0.3-m levels but later combined into three levels as some yielded very small collections. Levels defined were (1) 0 to 0.6 m (sherds mostly from the 0.3- to 0.6-m level); (2) 0.6 to 0.9 m; (3) 0.9 to 1.33 m.

Trench 12. A clearing rather than a trench. Room B (Lothrop, 1924, fig. 87) in Structure 25 was completely cleared of fallen roof debris. In the process an altar or bench was discovered, which almost covers the small room. It ranges from 0.32 to 0.36 m in height, and is 1.1 m wide. It is tempting to think of Room B as functioning as a household altar for the palace. A small ceramic sample was collected from above the floor.

Structure 45

Structure 45 is a small temple on a rocky knoll north of the Inner Enclosure. Just below and in front of it on the slope are four tiny shrines and a number of other structures. The knoll is almost bare of soil except for occasional pockets in the limestone. Surface sherds are abundant, almost entirely Buff Paste Censer, and a large sample was picked up during the 1954 field season. True trenching in this area was impossible, but "raking" out the soil pockets produced a good type sample of Tulum Buff Paste Censer. The raking operations along with clearing are summarized under Trenches 13, 14, 15, and 16.

Trench 13. The area between Structure 43, a shrine, and Structure 45 was evidently covered by a low terrace, most of which has eroded away. The remaining soil and fill were culled for sherds. The heaviest yield was along the west edge of the stairway, where a deep pocket yielded a large sample. Another concentration occurred in front of the shrine.

Trench 14. A small trench dug behind (south of) Structure 45. Soil here varied from 0.2 to 0.5 m in depth and yielded only a dozen sherds.

Trenches 15 and 16. Clearing operations. The shrines, Structures 39 and 40, have lost their roofs, which evidently collapsed inward on the floor. The debris was cleared out, and small sherd samples were collected and combined.

Summary of Structure 45 Trenches. None of our samples here are of chronological signifi-cance. Most of the sherds are of typical Tulum Buff Paste Censer and simply establish the use of the structures, and probably their construction, during the over-all period when this ware was being made.

Structure 54

Structure 54 is an isolated temple on a low platform base south of the Inner Enclosure. Three trenches were excavated.

Trench 17. Along the entire front (east) of the temple on both sides of the stairway, 1 m wide. The soil here is about 0.3 m deep, and sherd concentration was fairly heavy.

Trench 18. About 1 m wide, along the north face of the temple platform. Soil was approximately as deep as in Trench 17, and sherds were abundant. Curiously enough, a number of fragments of manos and metates were also picked up in this trench. Actually Structure 53, a low house platform, is just northwest, and the fragments probably represent debris thrown out from it.

Trench 19. A small trench dug into the fill of a terrace-like apron extending west just behind the temple platform. The terrace, which is not shown on Lothrop's plan or on ours, may be a low house base. A good sample was collected from the fill.

Here, as with Structure 45, the samples are from shallow deposits and provide only a mean date for the use of the structure.

Structure 35 (Cenote House)

Trenches dug around Structure 35 yielded some of the heaviest samples from the site, mainly Tulum Plain jars. Three trenches were excavated.

Trench 20. A meter wide, along almost the entire west side of the structure. Soil cover was typically scanty here, ranging from 0.1 to 0.4 m in depth, but a fair sample of pottery was picked up. An almost complete skeleton was uncovered directly on bedrock. Unfortunately it was disturbed by a laborer before it could be recorded. No grave furniture was associated with it, and it probably represents a sacrificial victim.

Trench 21. A small trench dug along the south or front edge of the structure west of the stairway. Soil cover was scanty, and sherds were few.

Trench 22. Trench 22 yielded the largest sample of any trench at Tulum. It extends along the east edge of the south annex of Structure 35 and is about 1 m wide. Soil here runs from 0.3 to 0.6 m in depth. Approximately at the south end of the trench, near the southeast corner of the annex, was uncovered a solid mass of pottery indurated in lime. Many of the sherds dissolved when attempts were made to wash them loose, but the bulk of the ceramic material was salvaged. It is mostly Tulum Plain ware jars plus Tulum Red, the latter yielding two restorable vessels (fig. 4,a,4). Below this mass of concreted pottery was a hole in the limestone leading into a narrow tunnel, which in turn entered the roof of the cenote underlying the structure. The mass of pottery had evidently been stuffed in to stop up this opening.

None of the trenches yielded stratigraphic information, and the concentration in Trench 22 is quite surely not refuse thrown out from the temple, but transported material. It did, however, provide my best sample of test sherds for Tulum Plain ware.

Structure 34

Structure 34 is a small, isolated palace north of the Structures 21-25 Group, east of and fronting on Main Street. Two trenches were dug along the platform of this structure.

Trench 23. On Main Street, running along the west edge of the structure from the stairway south to the southwest corner. Soil here was about 0.5 m deep, and sherds were abundant.

Trench 24. Along the back or east wall of the structure, 1.5 m wide. A fairly heavy sherd concentration occurred here, but the soil was shallower than in Trench 23.

Again, no deep deposits occurred around this structure, but the samples obviously represent trash from the occupation of the palace and serve to provide a mean date for it.

Structure 20

Structure 20 is situated across Main Street (on the west side) from the Fresco Temple and Structures 21-25 Group. It is a large (as Tulum buildings go) palace similar to Structures 21 and 25.

Trench 25. Along the street or east side of the structure, 1.5 m wide, and running from the stairway to the southeast corner of the structure. Soil here varied from 0.3 to 0.5 m in depth, and a fair ceramic sample was collected.

Trench 26. Along the back or west side of the structure, from the stairway to the southwest corner; 1.5 m wide. Soil here was surprisingly deep, running from 0.5 to 0.8 m, and sherds were abundant. A complete young adult male skeleton resting on bedrock was uncovered and recorded (fig. 13,e). The position of the skeleton gives the impression of a victim thrown down carelessly after death; a huge chunk of limestone rests on the small of the back, and no grave furniture was present. I suspect that the skeleton represents a sacrifice performed possibly to inaugurate the completion of the structure.

Structure 16. The Fresco Temple

Trenches excavated around this extremely important temple yielded disappointing results. The area has been kept clear of bush, and sherds have probably been culled by visitors for several decades. Six trenches were excavated all around the structure; each yielded a dozen or so sherds. Soil was scanty, running from 0.1 to 0.4 m. All sherds were lumped together and studied as a unit (Trenches 27, 28, 29, 30, 31). Another trench—Trench 32—was excavated into the building and the sample was separated.

Trench 32. Dug into the fill of the platform-like annex built along the east side of Structure 16. A small sherd sample was collected from the platform fill.

Inner Enclosure

The Main Plaza of Tulum, called by Lothrop the Inner Enclosure, was the scene of most intensive building at the site. It includes the main temple, the Castillo, along with a number of related structures. Fourteen excavations were conducted in and around this group. Nowhere was soil deep enough to permit arbitrary stratigraphy, and no masonry floors were encountered. In general, trenches dug on the outside of structures gave much better yields than those on the plaza side, with soil running from 0.2 to 0.6 m, the greater depth occurring only in occasional pockets in the trenches. Most of the plaza today is exposed bedrock with traces of neither soil nor floors. The trenches are summarized below.

Trench 33. A small 1-m-wide trench dug along the west edge of Structure 5, the Temple of the Diving God, from the stairway to the southwest corner. Soil here was less than 0.2 m deep, and sherds were rare.

Trench 34. Along the south edge of the Diving God temple; 1 m wide. Only a few sherds were collected, and the soil cover here is equally scanty.

Trench 35. North of the Temple of the Diving God the terrain slopes down to the "Port." On this slope, the depth of the soil is somewhat greater than on the plaza side of the structure, running 0.3 to 0.4 m to the west. The soil is mixed with fragments of limestone and pieces of masonry, representing building debris from the plaza and possibly modern clearing operations. A 1-m-wide trench was excavated along the entire north side, and a good sample, mainly censer ware, was collected.

Trench 36. On the plaza side (north) of Structure 10, a small palace. The trench, which measured 1 by 2 m, was excavated just west of the stairway. Soil cover and sherd yield were scanty.

Trench 37. A floor-clearing operation carried out in a part of Structure 10 (see fig. 2). Roof debris was cleared down to the floor of the structure, and a small sherd sample was collected. A long bench, 0.5 m high and 1.6 m wide, which probably runs all around the structure, was uncovered against the east wall.

Trench 38. Excavated along the entire south (back) of Structure 10; 1 m wide. Soil here was deeper than on the plaza side, running between 0.3 and 0.4 m, and pottery was abundant, yielding a figurine head (fig. 17,a) and a restorable vessel of Tulum Red Ware (fig. 4,a,3).

Trench 39. A floor-clearing operation carried out in Structure 2, a small temple on the north side of the Castillo and separated from it only by a 1-m-wide corridor. A broad band, about the width of the doorway, was cleared of fallen roof debris from the door back to the east (back) wall. An altar 0.3 m high, 0.95 m north-south, and 1.1 m east-west was uncovered against the back wall of the temple. Under the roof debris on the floor in front of the altar was a heavy concentration of sherds, mainly from two Tulum Black Paste Censer vessels with annular bases.

Trench 40. One meter wide, running along the entire south or back wall of Structure 9, the Temple of the Initial Series. Here the soil was from 0.3 to 0.4 m deep, and pottery was abundant.

Trench 41. Along the east side of Structure 9; 1 m wide. Sherds were abundant, and soil cover was about 0.3 m deep.

Trench 42. Between Structure 2 and the Castillo is a narrow, 0.3-m-wide space filled with fallen masonry debris. This was cleared out and a small pottery sample collected.

Trench 43. A continuation eastward of Trench 42 along the entire north side of the Castillo. It was widened to a full meter. Soil cover was scanty, but sherds abundant.

Trench 44. Another floor-clearing operation, this one carried out in Structure 4. The eastern half of the main room was cleared of debris, but few sherds were found.

Trench 45. The east annex of Structure 4 was completely cleared of roof debris. The entire room is occupied by an altar 0.26 m high. In the center of the altar against the back wall was a sunken, rectangular pit 0.33 by 0.23 m with plastered walls. It was evidently constructed for the insertion of the base of an incense burner, as it and the top of the altar near by were covered by sherds of a single Tulum Black Paste Censer vessel (fig. 8,d,1). The entire top of the altar between the pit and the door was covered by scattered sherds of the same ware.

Trench 46. A small trench dug along the back (east) wall of Structure 2. A small ceramic sample was collected.

Trench 47. One meter wide, excavated along the west edge of Structure 12, a low terrace-like platform. The trench ran from the stairway to the northwest corner. A fair sample of pottery was collected.

In summarizing the 14 excavations made in the Inner Enclosure a number of points may be noted. Trenches 39, 44, and 45 yielded valuable samples of pottery from the final phases of occupation of the plaza, since they were overlying altar tops or temple floors. Tulum Black Paste Censer, which dominates the samples, represents the final phases of the censer types developed at Tulum. The rest of the samples, especially those from outside the plaza, provide a total range of pottery wares and types from the start of the use of the center as a ceremonial precinct to its abandonment, but no arbitrary stratigraphy was defined to break down the chronology further. Trenches 35, 38, 40, 41, and 43 yielded first-class samples of Tulum ceramics and provided many well preserved, good type sherds, especially of Tulum Red and censer wares.

Market

Between Structures 25 and 33 is a large, open, level space that we have tentatively identified as the market place of the site (fig. 2). The soil here is deeper than anywhere else at Tulum and has a sandy texture, presumably due to hurricane floods from the sea. It is heavily stained with organic matter, however, and cultural refuse is abundant. To the west it is retained by a low stone wall defining the east edge of Main Street. To the east a second terrace face was discovered running parallel to that on Main Street, so that most of the area between the two structures seems to be included in a broad, low terrace. Three trenches were excavated in this area.

Trench 48. A small trench 1 by 2 m dug along the edge of the east terrace. Black stained sand to a depth of only 0.5 m was found here, and a few sherds.

Trench 49. On top of the terrace and about 15 m north of Structure 25. Trench 49 was a 2 by 2 m exploratory cut that revealed some 1.4 m of cultural deposit resting on bedrock. The first 0.6 m was black stained sand, and below it was 0.5 m of terrace fill made up of chunks of limestone and village refuse. With the discovery of deep refuse it was decided to excavate another trench near by and to separate material by cultural and arbitrary stratigraphic levels.

Trench 50. This trench lies 0.3 m south of Trench 49. Three levels were defined: Level 1, 0 to 0.3 m; Level 2, 0.3 to 0.6 m; and Level 3, 0.6 to 1 m. · Levels 1 and 2 were humus-stained sand; Level 3 was rock fill. Cultural refuse was abundant, particularly in Level 2; it included pottery, bone, and especially shell.

CERAMIC CHRONOLOGY OF TULUM

Initial survey of the pottery made it evident that at Tulum but a single ceramic complex and a single chronological period are represented. The chief problem then was concerned with the division of this period into phases; by extensive trenching near most of the major structures of the site and stratigraphic excavations where deep deposits occurred I had hopes of working out the chronology of Tulum in detail. Before the results of this trenching are discussed, a few general observations are pertinent to the problem of Tulum chronology.

First, deep deposits at Tulum are such a rarity that arbitrary stratigraphy was seldom possible. The soil deposits average 0.2 to 0.5 m in depth over the site as a whole, and only in the "Market" are there any suitable for arbitrary stratigraphy. In the Inner Enclosure, where, because of the complexity and obvious importance of the group, stratified floors might be hoped for, from 0 to 0.3 m of soil, most of it building rubble, rests directly on bedrock, with no signs of any masonry floors at all. Our best stratigraphy from Tancah was from the plaza side of important religious structures; the lack of such stratigraphy at Tulum suggests an extremely short period of occupation.

The ceramic assemblage at Tulum, in basic outline, continues from the lowest levels of the trenches to the top. There are no important changes either in vessel shapes or in basic wares. The pottery forms a well defined complex which includes three principal wares, Tulum Red, Tulum Plain, and Tulum Buff Paste Censer, plus a few sherds of Mayapan Black-on-cream and V Fine Orange. I am proposing the name Tulum Complex or Tulum Period for this assemblage. It evidently was contemporary with the Mayapan Period in central Yucatan, was in vogue on the east coast only two centuries at most, and enjoyed a huge spatial range running from Holbox to Chetumal, or the entire east coast of the Peninsula. The only possibility, then, in working out phases within this period lies in percentile variations between vessel forms or possibly from ware to ware. Complicating the latter possibility are the varied functions of buildings lying in the vicinity of the trenches. For example, the sample culled from trenches near Structure 45 is almost entirely Buff Paste Censer, a reasonable finding since this building is an isolated shrine. Trenches near palace platforms yield a high percentage of Tulum Red, which was probably a "Sunday best" household ware.

Before the results of the trench analysis are discussed a few points might be made with respect to Lothrop's chronological phases, which are based on architectonic stratigraphy.

On the basis of the documentary material, and using the then current Morley-Spinden correlation, Lothrop (1924, pp. 168-170) postulated the following major time divisions for the area:

Colonization Period	A.D.	433- 689	Contemporary with Great Period in Peten.
Dark Ages	A.D.	689- 985	
League of Mayapan	A.D.	985-1201	The New Empire or florescence of culture in northern Yucatan.
Toltec Period	A.D.	1201-1458	Period of Mexican influence and dominance of Mayapan; period of maximum prosperity on the east coast.
Final Period			Cultural disorganization, war, famine.

He assigned the bulk of the architecture of the sites he studied, and all the structures within the wall at Tulum, to the Toltec Period. He assigned many of the buildings at Tancah and Xelha to the preceding League Period.

On the basis of building stratigraphy at Tulum he broke down the Toltec Period into four phases, which are summarized in table 1. The Toltec Period architectural complex on the east coast includes serpent columns and balustrades, sloping or battered bases of temple walls, platform mounds with colonnades, and flat beam-and-masonry roofs. Distinguished clearly from this is the architectural complex found at Tancah and Xelha, which lacks these features, all buildings having corbeled roofs; also at those two sites are found three-member moldings and roof combs.

Lothrop's ideas about Quintana Roo chronology are no longer acceptable, even on the documentary side, and certainly they are not supported by archaeological evidence, but his architectural sequence is based on clear-cut stratigraphy and is undoubtedly sound. We found that the sharp

TABLE 1. BUILDING STRATIGRAPHY AT TULUM (after Lothrop)

	Walls	Panel	Ceiling	Molding

A B C

	Walls	Panel	Ceiling	Molding
GROUP I:				
11, 16, 59	Thick	Touching molding	Vaulted	A
1h, 9, 45, 57	Thick	Touching molding	Vaulted	B
GROUP II:				
1c-f, 1g, 2, 3, 4, 5, 54	Medium	Touching molding	Flat	C
10, 21a-c	Medium	Touching molding	Flat	B
GROUP III:				
20, 21de, 34, 35	Medium	Below molding	Flat	B
25	Medium	Below molding	Flat	A
GROUP IV:				
1ab, 16, 55, 56	Thin	Below molding	Vaulted	A

distinctions in architecture between Tancah and Tulum are accompanied by equally distinct ceramic assemblages. Tancah was apparently abandoned as a main center, however, about the date Lothrop suggests as its beginning. His dating for Tulum, on the other hand, is likely to be very close, although not because of its ties with Chichen Itza, as he believed, but rather because of its connection with Mayapan, which the evidence now dates as post-Chichen Itza and as roughly spanning the time horizon that Lothrop suggested for Tulum.

Here we are interested principally in Lothrop's breakdown of the Tulum architectural period into its four phases, which I had originally hoped to be able to correlate with ceramic phases. For this reason trenches were dug along many structures, and a number of refuse pits were dug, using arbitrary stratigraphy combined with some building stratigraphy.

For example, if our deep stratigraphic tests revealed a consistent order of frequency of wares or forms, then trenches along buildings of different architectural phases should reflect those variations. In some places this reasoning would not apply, because different rooms of a single building correlated with different architectural phases and so the rubbish in the shallow soil off the edge of the platform would obviously be mixed. Many buildings, however, seem to fit into a single period. Structures 45 and 9, for instance, are early, although 9 is part of a larger unit, the Inner Enclosure, in which building went on throughout the occupation of Tulum, and that structure is not too good as a test. Structures 54 and 10 are intermediate, 10 again presenting problems as it is part of the Inner Enclosure complex. Structures 34, 35, and 25 are all late.

One of the likeliest areas of the site to test this method is the Structures 21-25 Group, where we have an easily defined series of architectural phases, and also three stratigraphic trenches either near by or off the edges of the structures. Having already discussed the architectural history of the complex, I will simply review briefly the trenches and probable stratigraphic relationship.

A. Stratigraphic trenches with more than one level defined by arbitrary limits. This group includes Trenches 4, 11, and 40.

B. Trenches 9, 10. These are unstratified; they are situated in front of Structure 21, probably the first part of the total architectural complex to be built. They should include both the earliest and the latest pottery phases.

C. Trenches 5, 6, 7, 12. All but 12 include samples from on top of the filled-in original courtyard; 12 is from a room in Structure 25. All sherds are from on top of the latest floors of the terrace and building and should yield the latest ceramic material of the complex.

D. Trench 8. This is from inside the fill of the buried platform which once faced the original courtyard on the east; it should have unmixed material of the earliest ceramic phase of the complex.

Study of table 2, which shows the frequency of wares and shapes, leads to the following observations.

(a) No forms are limited to any one level or postulated phase, and no absolute time markers can be pointed out.

(b) Evidence indicates that Tulum Red is somewhat dominant over Tulum Plain in the earlier material, and that the reverse is true for the later. On the other hand, the actual percentile relations are far from consistent, and we cannot define phases on the basis of absolute percentile variations for testing outside of the complex. As a matter of fact, it is rather difficult to separate Tulum Plain from Tulum Red that has lost its slip, for shapes and even paste overlap, and conceivably erosion of the later material could be responsible for the variation.

(c) Coarse Paste jars seem to tend toward the later end of our group chronology, and basal flange bowls toward the earlier; incision may be a little more common toward the beginning than later on; and Mayapan Black-on-cream may be more heavily represented during the beginning phases of growth of the group.

These remarks just about sum up the variation in the sample, and the net result is rather disappointing. I do not think that the Tulum Period can be broken down into constituent phases on this basis.

To demonstrate further the lack of effective seriation I will review briefly the samples from other structures on the site.

Structure 45. According to Lothrop, Structure 45 is one of the earliest at Tulum (see table 1). Unfortunately our sample does not permit comparison with the Structures 21-25 Group sequence since it is almost entirely Buff Paste Censer. Tulum Red and Tulum Plain together do not number more than 41 sherds in a total sample of over 500 in Trench 13. The sample does include a sherd from a basal flange bowl of Tulum Red ware.

Structure 54 dates with Lothrop's Phase 2 and should compare with our earliest material from the Structures 21-25 Group. The results for Trenches 17 and 18 do not check at all with our postulated phases. Of course all the first structures built at Tulum were probably in use throughout the history of the site, and it is precisely the earliest buildings that are least susceptible of dating by our method.

Structure 35 seems to date entirely with Lothrop's Phase 3. For this building our findings check closely with the results from the Structures 21-25 Group. Tulum Plain outnumbers Tulum Red nearly 6 to 1, and basal flange bowls are very rare. On the other hand, incision is not

TABLE 2. FREQUENCIES OF WARES AND SHAPES FROM STRATIGRAPHIC TRENCHES AT TULUM

Stratigraphic Trenches	Levels	Bowls (Tulum Red Ware)							Jars (Tulum Red Ware)								Miscellaneous (Tulum Red Ware)				Totals		Tulum Plain		Tulum Censer		Mayapan Black on Cream	V Fine Orange	Eroded	Total All Sherds
		Basal break, plain	Basal flange	Hemispherical, plain	Basal break, incised	Hemispherical, incised	Miscellaneous body	Supports	Flaring rim	Direct rim, plain	Direct rim, incised	Bases	Handles	Shoulder-neck	Miscellaneous body	Incised body	Coarse Paste	Other slip colors	Exotic	Unclassified body	Total Tulum Red	Total Incised Sherds	Jar	Bowl	Buff Paste	Black Paste				
1, 2		3						6	2	1	1	1	1							40	55	1	74		15		8			152
3		12		1				8	11	7	1	7	3	9			1	88		267	415	1	453		11		98	1	33	1,011
4	1	2						7	2	4		1		2		1		4	1	50	72	1	197	1	13		13	3	10	309
4	2		1	2*				2	6	1		1						7		70	90		97		3		7	1		198
5		8			1			5	2					9				14	6		45	1	25		35				4	109
6		4			1		37									30	50	32	1		155	1	137		6		1			299
7									1					2			4	4		13	24		38		4					66
8		2	1											5				4		47	59		64		2		40		33	198
9								2	1	5			3	1		1	6	3		3	25	1	42		79			2		148
10		3		2				2	1	7				2		1	21	26	5	94	162	3	45	9	45	68	33	4		366
11	1							2	1			1		3			6	17		30	60		42		6		1		9	118
11	2	3			1						1			1		5	2	16		68	97	6	47	1			1		8	154
11	3		3						1	2		3			7	2		11		21	50	2	26		1		3			80
12		1	1					1	1						2					55	60		64		2					126
13			1					4	1											12	18		23		474			1		516
15, 16		1												2				3		22	28		37		25			1		91
17		6						6	1	7	1		3	4				13		72	113	1	207		73		15	1		409
18								2			1					1		3		33	40	2	130		13		1			184
19		3		1		1		4	2	3			4	1				5		126	150	1	152		8		14	1		325
20			2					2	2	4	1			4				9		56	80	1	130		3		7	2		222
21							1	2	1											18	22		76		10		6	1		115
22		2						5	5	18	6		1	1	10	8	1	46	1	105	209	14	1151		4		31	7		1,402
23		4	1		2			10	3					6			7	82		76	191	2	109		17		22	2		341
24								3		2				1				39		32	77		91		4		11	1	10	194
25		2	1	1				3	3	8		1		11	2		18	26		130	206		151	2	22		5	3		389
26		7						4	1		2		3	1		2	1	13		45	79	4	75		24		5	1		184
27-31								2	1								1	18	2	39	63		61		60		6	2		192
32			1					1	1											15	17		23		39			3		82
33, 34		1						2	1							2				14	20	2	25		9		1			55
35								2	1					3				18		29	49		122		47		14	3		235
36, 37					3			4	1					3						34	45	3	56		3				4	108
38		4	3	1*	1			13	3	3	1		7	7				44	1	101	189	2	257		58		1	4		509
39																				25	25		17		6	66	9	1		124
40		4	1					1	1	1	1	2	2	4			2	12		60	91	1	152		39		9			291
41		5	1	4				13		8	2	1	7	8	5		1	71	5	233	364	2	333		118		20	8		843
42		1	1					3						4						14	23		13		83		1			120
43					1	1		4	2	6		1	3	2			30	27	1	103	181	2	223		105		53	2		564
44, 45								1		5				1		1	1			13	9	1	2			135				146
46		2						5	3											13	23		9		28		2			62
47		1							1					1		1		2		32	35		121		26		4			186
48		1							1					1		1		1		33	38		3		5		4			50
49		8	6	2				8	1	7		5	5	8	13			30	2	138	233		154		1		45	6		439
50	1							1									4			26	31		51		1		3		22	108
50	2	8						1	5	1	1		2				6	34		41	99	1	137		2		42	1	70	351
50	3	4						1	3			1				5		18		40	72		40				13	1		126
Ext		3		1				2	1	1		2	1	6				10		54	81	1	78				22		13	194
Total		103	23	13	6	9	38	142	66	105	18	25	51	95	86	24	162	750	25	2529	4270	57	5560	13	1529	269	570	64	216	12,491

* Grater bowl

particularly rare, nor is Mayapan Black-on-cream, and Coarse Paste jars are almost absent.

Structure 34. It can be seen from table 2 that wares and shapes from Trenches 23 and 24 differ markedly from those from trenches about Structure 35, a finding that does not tend to reinforce our postulated phases.

Structures 20, 34, 35, and 25 form a group all dating with Lothrop's Phase 3, and all should present similar ceramic seriation with tendencies toward late datings. Trenches 25 and 26 by Structure 20 do not justify this hope, and thus we find again a lack of correlation.

These are the only isolated buildings that were fitted by Lothrop into his sequence of architectural forms. Our trenches from shallow soil deposits along the outer edge of buildings surrounding the Inner Enclosure obviously cannot be used with our method, since the enclosure was the main ceremonial center from start to finish of the occupation at Tulum and the samples are mixed.

The net result of so much discussion and comparison seems hardly worth the effort, but I think it does establish with certainty that Tulum represents a site that had a single major ceramic phase and was probably occupied for a comparatively short period. I should suggest that Lothrop's dating be considered an outside estimate, and that Tulum did not enjoy more than two centuries of life. The only possibility of internal dating, then, seems to be that done by Lothrop purely on constructional levels and architectural forms.

One definite variation in the Tulum ceramic assemblage, however, undoubtedly has chronological significance. The above-floor samples from Trenches 39, 45, and 46 (Structures 2 and 4) yielded a heavy percentage of Tulum Black Paste Censer. A few sherds were also picked up in unstratified mixed deposits, but in general the ware seems to be limited to the final use of religious structures before the complete abandonment of the site. It did not occur in any of our deep stratigraphic pits. It probably dates from the final 50 years or so before the Spanish Conquest, and I suspect that Tulum had already been abandoned as a population center when it came into vogue.

Curiously enough, not a single sherd of pottery of the assemblages found at Tancah in constructional levels and no Initial Series Period pottery of any kind was collected at Tulum, although 50 stratigraphic trenches and over 70 settlement-pattern trenches were dug at the site. The conclusion seems clear that in spite of the nearness of Tancah no settlement or construction occurred at Tulum earlier than the Tulum Period. This brings up the problem of the stela with an Initial Series date reported first by Stephens and read by Lothrop (1924, p. 42) as a 9.13.10.0.0 7 Ahau 3 Cumhu date. The stela was evidently set up in front of Structure 9. There are no buildings or pottery from Tulum so early, and I believe that it was probably moved from Tancah, possibly in pre-Conquest times.

4. NORTHERN QUINTANA ROO

During the 1954 season some 40 sites, including Tancah and Tulum, in northern Quintana Roo were visited and small test excavations were made (frontispiece). Rough maps and plans and fairly detailed descriptions have been published in a previous report (Sanders, 1955), which should be referred to for more detailed information on the sites. Here I will simply discuss the pottery samples and evaluate them chronologically. The sites studied may be grouped into the following geographical regions.

NORTH-COAST SITES

North-coast sites include those along the Laguna de Yalahau (Yuukluuk, Vista Alegre, and Chiquila) and on the stretch of east coast north of Puerto Morelos (including the sites of Cancun, El Meco, Cocal 1, and Cocal 2). This grouping of sites differs from my 1955 report, which was prepared before the pottery had been studied. Most of the ceramic material collected was post-Classic, tying in closely with the Mayapan Period in central Yucatan and the Tulum Period farther south along the east coast. Chiquila Censer is the type censer for the Tulum Period in this area. It has similarities to both Tulum Buff Paste Censer and Mayapan censer, but the reddish colors, often brick red, characteristic of paste and surface distinguish it from the typical buff Tulum censer. Also the female figurines associated with this ware are lacking at Tulum, and slipping (red) along with incised decoration is more common here than farther south. The dividing line between Tulum and Chiquila Censers on the east coast lies between Cocal 2 and Mulchi, if our sampling can be considered definitive.

Along with Chiquila Censer, Tulum Red and unslipped wares occur in minor percentages, and so does V Fine Orange, which is the Mayapan type.

At two sites, Chiquila and Vista Alegre, Classic materials occur also. The site samples are reviewed below.

Yuukluuk

As described in my 1955 report, this is a small one-shrine site on the south shore of Holbox Island; only the bases of the walls and floor are intact.

Wall and roof debris was cleaned off the temple floor to obtain a superficial sample. In the excavation an altar was uncovered against the back (south) wall of the temple. A good sample, mainly of censer ware, was picked up from these floor-clearing operations. A second excavation at the base of the stairway produced only a few sherds.

Four sherds of Tulum Red ware jars (three rims and a handle) were collected, and one rim of a Tulum Plain jar. Finally a V Fine Orange support (bulbous with rattle) was also found (fig. 7,a,22). All the rest of the sherds, about 90 per cent of the sample, are Chiquila Censer. The censer sample includes 24 rims, part of a human face, 2 figurine feet, and a complete ladle-type censer handle.

Cancun Island

Group 1. A series of small trenches were dug along the plaza sides of Structures 1, 2, and 4.

189

Most of the sample came from Structure 4. All samples were lumped together, and no arbitrary or natural stratigraphy was defined as all trenches were shallow and no constructional levels were encountered. The plaza was probably unpaved, perhaps covered with white sand.

Almost the entire lot was Chiquila Censer, and it included 39 rims (from tall jarlike forms similar to the complete vessel from El Meco), 418 miscellaneous body sherds, and 21 adornos and figurine parts. Also collected were 3 V Fine Orange sherds and 54 Tulum Buff Paste Censer sherds.

Group 3. (San Miguel.) Several small trenches were dug along the edges of house platforms. All samples were small, and trenches shallow.

The following wares were collected in this sample: V Fine Orange, 16 sherds; Tulum Plain jars, 122 sherds (15 rims, 1 strap handle included; some sherds show traces of red slip and are probably Tulum Red); Tulum Red, 25 sherds (includes 2 supports and 6 bowl rims); Yucatan Slate, 3 badly eroded sherds; 120 sherds of very badly eroded brick-red ware which has a medium coarse paste and an occasional trace of slip. All the last are small rim and body sherds and almost impossible to classify; some are probably Chiquila Censer, but a few of the rims are Tulum Plain jars in form, and some may even be eroded Tulum Red.

All the samples from Cancun, Cocal 1, and Cocal 2 are so eroded by the humid saline beach deposits in which they occur that often shape is the only clear feature of the vessels; and in shape there is considerable cross-over from one post-Classic ware to another. What is clear at Cancun is the strong Tulum influence and lack of Classic Period wares. In shape, paste, and surface, the censer ware coincides exactly with our sample from the Chiquila type site.

El Meco

Trench 1. Trench 1 was excavated at the foot of the Castillo stairway and carried to bedrock. A good sample, mainly of censer ware, was collected from it.

Two sherds of Tulum Red, including an incised jar shoulder, 1 V Fine Orange bowl rim, and 12 sherds of Tulum Buff Paste Censer were collected from this trench, most of which probably represent imports from Tulum. The rest of the sample was Chiquila Censer, among which was a restorable vessel (see fig. 15,f), a typical pedestal-base, straight-wall censer with pierced and incised walls and pierced base. Also occurring in the censer sample were typical Chiquila type rims, figurine faces, arms, feet, fans, plumes, and back ornaments. A large figurine fragment was recovered, evidently a headdress. In all, 26 sherds besides the restored vessel were classified as Chiquila Censer.

Trench 2. A series of trenches were excavated along the plaza edge of the east and south platforms. The few sherds collected were lumped together in a single sample; it covered a greater range of sherds than the Trench 1 sample and included a few Classic wares. V Fine Orange was well represented, 7 sherds in all, mostly from simple bowls; 5 sherds were classified as Tulum Red; 5, as Vista Alegre Striated; 2, as Yucatan Slate basal break bowls (1 the typical east-coast form); Tulum Plain was represented by 27 sherds; Tulum Buff Paste Censer, by 30; and Chiquila Censer, by 50.

The data indicate that the site of El Meco clearly falls in the Tulum Period, and there is a distinct possibility of a Classic occupation level as well.

Cocal 1

Only a pit is left where the temple described by Escalona Ramos (1946, p. 541) once stood.

Sherds were abundant in the floor and wall of the pit, and a large sample of pottery was collected by scraping down the walls. It is entirely Chiquila Censer of the Tulum Period. It consists of 302 sherds, including 37 rims and numerous adornos and figurine fragments, all badly eroded.

Cocal 2

A small sherd sample was collected from a trench dug along the east side of the temple platform, and another from the debris cleared from part of the temple floor. Of the 56 sherds taken from the site, 55 are Chiquila Censer, including a typical handle from a ladle censer and typical Chiquila type rims and adornos. The other sherd, a pierced base, seems to be Tulum Black Paste Censer.

Vista Alegre

Vista Alegre is a fairly large site with several big pyramids and platforms and at least a dozen house platforms of considerable size. It evidently had a long occupational period, as our sherd samples prove; it has a fair amount of ceramic depth (more than 1 m in spots), and is the type site for the ware I am calling Vista Alegre Striated. One of the trenches yielded arbitrary stratigraphy.

Trench 1 was the most productive excavation, with three arbitrary 0.3-m levels defined. It was 3 by 1 m and dug along the edge of a house platform.

Trenches 2, 3, and 4 were also dug along house platforms, but only small samples were found from shallow deposits. They were studied together and give a good idea of total range of types for the site. See table below.

	Trench 1			Trenches 2, 3, 4
	Level 1	Level 2	Level 3	
Tulum Red	31	0	0	9
Tulum Plain	117	0	0	23
V Fine Orange	2	0	1	3
Mayapan Black-on-cream	25	14*	4	9
Chiquila Censer	27	0	0	5
Brown slip	20			
Red slip	4			
No slip	3			
Vista Alegre Striated	44	83	55	25
Tancah Plain	12	15†	0	
Regional Polychrome	0	4	3	
Yucatan Slate (Medium Paste)	0	9	8	5
Tentative identifications and miscellaneous sherds				
Fine Paste Gray, polished	0	4	3	
Regional Polychrome	0	10	0	
Puuc or Chichen Red	0	2	0	11
Black slipped ware	0	0	0	11
Plain unslipped jars (related to Tulum Plain)	0	0	0	13
Total	258	141	74	114

*Some of these may be Yucatan Slate ware.
† Mostly restricted orifice bowls.

The trenches show a fairly long period of occupation. The Regional Polychrome sherds are Tepeu in type, and no basal flange bowls were found; therefore the site occupation probably starts with the Yucatecan Florescent and runs on to the Tulum Period. Of interest is the heavy Tulum Period representation in the superficial level with evidence of the same suddenness of appearance as at Tancah. The lower levels are dominated by Vista Alegre Striated. Certain trends can be seen from Trench 1. Vista Alegre Striated increases from top to bottom, markedly so from Level 1 to Level 2. Yucatan Slate appears in Level 2 and increases downward in frequency, and Mayapan Black-on-cream decreases sharply in Level 3. Some of the last may really be Yucatan Slate; the condition of the sherds makes identification difficult.

The site of Vista Alegre may be the Conquest Period site of Conil. The heavy Tulum Period occupation on top strengthens the possibility.

Chiquila

At the site of Chiquila good building stratigraphy was discovered, especially at the Great Platform. This is a big square platform surmounted by two smaller platforms. Two trenches were excavated on top of the main platform.

Trench 1. Running along the south edge of the east summit platform. The trench was excavated to a depth of 1 m in two levels. The upper level consisted of 0.3 m of loose black top soil in which sherds were abundant. No preserved floor was found, but the top soil shifts abruptly to the main platform fill of small chunks of limestone at about the 0.3-m point. All sherds from below this level were taken out separately. The samples sorted into two clear-cut ceramic complexes as follows:

	Level 1	Level 2
Chiquila Censer	110	6
Tancah Red	4	0
Chiquila Variegated	3	40
Tancah Plain-Striated	0	29
Regional Polychrome	7	26
Total	124	101

Of the Regional Polychrome from Level 2, one sherd is from a typical basal flange bowl. The complete lack of striated wares of any kind, especially Vista Alegre, is significant. The Level 2 sample seems to be mostly Late Regional; the absence of Tancah Red is probably more apparent than real, since the Chiquila sample was studied before Tancah Red and Variegated were defined. Most of the small body sherds were disposed of at the end of the season, only selected rims and bases being kept. Of those, one is Tancah Red, and probably a few of the body sherds were also this ware. The predominance of Variegated is clear, however, and indicates the chronological position noted. The Level 2 sample is homogeneous and seems to represent a single ceramic phase as the complete lack of Yucatan Slate and Vista Alegre Striated indicates.

Level 1 is typically post-Classic.

Trench 2. Excavated along the east side of the west platform on top of Platform 1. The trench proved to be extraordinarily rich; it evidently cut through the temple refuse heap. The base of the mound was covered by a 0.4-m-deep deposit of almost solid pottery in loose black top soil, which formed a talus to the slope of the structure. Below it was a layer of small-stone fill of the main platform, again with no preserved floor capping it, and below this a layer of large chunks of limestone fill. The trench was excavated to a total depth of 1 m, and the ceramic sample was separated in two levels as at Trench 1.

The extraordinarily rich sample from Level 1 provided the type sample for Chiquila Censer, including some 840 sherds. All but a few were of the censer ware, although 16 sherds had red or brown slips. The problem of identification of this ware is dealt with and it is described exhaustively in later sections. Most of the sherds are from tall, annular-based jars or vases with attached full-length female figurines. The sample included 70 rim sherds from annular bases or mouths, 28 body sherds with the filet-punched band design, 18 incised body sherds, 30 adornos from figurines (plumes, fans, shoulder wings, buttons, etc.), 55 large body sherds, 5 figurine feet, 7 fragments of arms and legs, 1 crown, 7 hands, 5 vessel supports (1 is a typical Tulum support), 1 hand holding a bowl of copal incense, 1 bird effigy, 1 alligator effigy, 2 ladle handles, 4 human-face sherds, 5 large sherds including breasts and arms of female figurines, and 16 slipped sherds; the balance consisted of small body sherds.

Level 2 yielded very few sherds, and my sample is somewhat mixed as it includes 23 censer sherds. Other wares included 4 Chiquila Variegated, 5 Regional Polychrome, 4 Tancah Plain, and 2 sherds of restricted orifice bowls, not striated but with Vista Alegre shaped rims. Most of the sherds came from the small-stone fill at the top of the level.

As was described in the earlier survey report (Sanders, 1955, p. 190), a chultun was uncovered in the trench (fig. 14,j), the capstone being just about at the line of junction between Levels 1 and 2. In cleaning out the soil accumulation from the chultun a few tiny jade and shell beads were collected and 6 sherds, of which 3 were identified (1 Chiquila Variegated, 2 Regional Polychrome).

Trench 3. A trench along the west side of Mound 2, a big pyramid situated about 150 m northeast of Platform 1. Two 0.3-m levels were defined; a badly preserved masonry floor separated the levels at about 0.3 m but was useless for stratigraphy because of its condition. The levels, therefore, are more or less arbitrary.

	Level 1	Level 2
Chiquila Censer	25	0
Vista Alegre Striated	0	10
Chiquila Variegated	1	0
Tancah Plain-Striated	16	0
Regional Polychrome	4	6
Miscellaneous unslipped red ware	0	35
Total	46	51

COZUMEL ISLAND SITES

Although many of the sites excavated on Cozumel Island yielded insufficient samples for dating, two (San Miguel and Aguada Grande) provided abundant samples, and three (San Gervasio, Punta Islote, and Celerain 1), fair samples. The data are summarized below.

San Miguel

No structures of this site described by Escalona Ramos are standing today. Our sample is equivalent to a surface collection, having been culled from disturbed refuse deposits. The sample was abundant and yielded our heaviest concentration of Yucatan Slate ware found in either field season. It breaks down as tabulated.

Tulum Red	25
V Fine Orange	4
Chiquila Censer	10
Vista Alegre Striated	119 (30 rims)
Tancah Plain (restricted orifice)	20 (5 rims)
Regional Polychrome	10
Yucatan Slate (Medium Paste)	267 (total)
Basal break bowls	
Dark brown slip	76 (18 rims)
Light brown slip	65 (8 rims)
Orange-red slip	22
Orange-brown slip	32 (2 rims)
Cream slip	32 (5 rims)
Basins	12 (2 rims)
Black-on-slate	28 (2 rims)
Yucatan Thin Slate	11 (total)
Dark brown slip	1 (rim)
Light brown slip	9 (7 rims)
Orange-brown slip	1 (rim)
Tentative and miscellaneous wares	
Unstriated body (probably Vista Alegre Striated)	220
Coarse plain (probably Tancah Plain)	230
Fine paste unslipped buff	1 reconstructable bowl
Total	917

The Vista Alegre Striated sample is identical to that from Vista Alegre and is equally well represented. Yucatan Slate is more common than at Vista Alegre; possibly our sample from San Miguel is slightly earlier. There is, however, a light post-Classic occupation at San Miguel, as the Tulum Red and censer sherds show.

Aguada Grande

Aguada Grande is one of the most interesting sites on Cozumel Island, both in its settlement pattern and in its ceramic assemblage.

Trench 1. Trench 1 consisted of clearing the roof and wall debris from the floor of Temple A (fig. 12,j). The floor was completely cleared, and a low altar was uncovered against the back wall. In the rubble and especially on the floor around the altar was one of the most extraordinary ceramic dumps found in the two seasons; some 1050 sherds were collected, almost all from a coarse, soft, crumbly ware that we have called Aguada Grande Censer. The only other ware represented was Tulum Buff Paste Censer, of which 45 sherds were collected. The time position of Tulum, along with the lack at that site of Aguada Grande Censer in its most specific form (as represented here), suggests strongly that it is post-Tulum and perhaps even post-Conquest. Tulum Black Paste Censer with close paste and surface similarities occurs always on the floors of the latest building levels at Tulum, and here at Aguada Grande the sample is mainly a post-constructional assemblage. If our dating of Aguada Grande Censer ware is correct, Aguada Grande must have been one of the last strongholds of paganism on the island, to judge from the quantity of pottery.

Trench 2. A small trench dug along the base of the stairway of Temple D. In general the bedrock was only 0.3 m deep, but in one area there was a small round pit in the limestone, literally stuffed with sherds, where the trench extended down for nearly 1 m. No levels were taken, unfortunately, and so our sample is mixed; most of the sample was Aguada Grande Censer, but a good representation of a number of other wares was found as well:

Tulum Buff Paste Censer	40
Aguada Grande Censer	902
Vista Alegre Striated	2
Tancah Plain	8
Regional Polychrome	31
Yucatan Slate and Thin Slate	10
Puuc Red	1
Total	994

The evidence suggests a Classic and a Tulum Period occupation of the site as well as heavy use during the Colonial Period. One of the buildings, Temple C, has a typical Maya corbeled roof; the others, flat beam-and-masonry roofs. The possibility seems strong that there was a small Classic shrine (Temple C) at Aguada Grande which was expanded into a ceremonial center and plaza during the Tulum Period and was heavily reused for pagan ritual in post-Conquest times. Test trenches were also excavated along Platforms 1 and 2, but little refuse was encountered and few sherds.

San Gervasio

San Gervasio is the most impressive site we visited on the island. It actually would be classed as small in comparison with those in richer areas, but it may have been the main center of the island during the Tulum Period, to which it seems mainly to relate. Escalona Ramos points out that the architecture suggests that Structure 3 (fig. 13,m,n), with a corbeled roof and exceptionally fine masonry, is Classic in style, and the rest are typical post-Classic structures with roofs supported by columns.

Trench 1. A 1-m-wide trench running along the entire plaza side of Structure 4, at the base of the main stairway, which was also cleared of debris. A second trench, 1.5 m wide, about the width of the stairway, was carried from the stairway back to the west wall, and building debris was cleared to the floor (fig. 13,o). An altar, or bench, was uncovered, running along the back (west) wall (fig. 13,f). Sherds from both these trenches were lumped together for laboratory analysis. The following wares were represented:

Tulum Red	27
Tulum Plain	54
V Fine Orange	2
Mayapan Black-on-cream	5
Tulum Buff Paste and Chiquila Censer	25
Tulum Black Paste Censer	33
Tancah Plain	45
Total	191

Trench 2. Excavated in rubble behind Structure 3. A very small sample was found:

Tulum Red	16
Tulum Plain	10

Chiquila Censer	1
Tulum Black Paste Censer	35
Tancah Plain	8
Total	70

El Cedral

From a shallow trench dug behind (east side of) Structure 1 and a floor-clearing operation in Structure 3, a small ceramic sample was obtained which indicates a Late Classic and a post-Classic occupation at El Cedral. Wares were as follows:

Tulum Red	1
Tulum Buff Paste Censer	1
Tulum Black Paste Censer	12
Tancah Striated	9
Tancah Plain	13
Regional Polychrome	1
Yucatan Slate	22
Total	59

Celerain 1

The floor debris from the front room was cleared out in this single-shrine site, and a sample of 100 Tulum Black Paste Censer sherds was picked up, mostly from a single vessel with filet band decoration and annular base.

Punta Islote

Punta Islote is a small two-building site. One of the structures was of palace type with beam-and-masonry roof. The floor debris was cleared from about half of the building, but few sherds were found. Other excavations were made along the bases of both stairways of Temple 1, Temple of the Four Directions (figs. 13,g,h,i), and a fair sample was picked up including pottery, jade and coral beads, and part of a chert knife. The wares were as follows:

Tulum Buff Paste Censer	3
Tulum Black Paste Censer	90 (60 burned brick red)
Yucatan Slate	6
Puuc Red (tentative identification)	9
Total	108

Celerain 2

From clearing of floor debris of the little shrine at this site (fig. 13,j) a small pottery sample was collected. Of it, 31 sherds were Tulum Black Paste Censer and 57 were of a coarse, thin, buff unslipped ware, badly eroded, which probably is Tulum Plain and Buff Paste Censer mixed.

Las Grecas

A small sample picked up from a trench along the base of the main building stairway included 121 sherds of Tulum Black Paste Censer, 2 sherds of Tulum Red, and 6 of Tulum Plain.

Arrecife Site

Trenching in and around this site (figs. 12,k; 13,k,l), a single complex of buildings, revealed no important concentrations of pottery. Only 31 sherds, all small, were picked up in these trenches. Tulum Black Paste Censer numbered 25, Tulum Censer 3, Chiquila Censer 2, and Tulum Red ware 1.

Trenching at the sites of Punta Molas, El Real (fig. 12,l), and Janan (fig. 14,a) yielded only a few sherds each, none identifiable.

EAST-COAST SITES

The distinction between east coast and north coast is in part geographical, in part cultural. Tulum Buff Paste Censer is replaced by Chiquila Censer ware between Mulchi and Cocal 2, and, referring to earlier times, Tancah Variegated and Tancah Striated occur mainly south of this point and Chiquila Variegated and Vista Alegre Striated north of it. It is only during the Late Classic that we find a breaking down of these regional divisions. Small to fair ceramic samples were collected from Mulchi, Kilometer 35, Xelha, Ak 1, Palmol, and Palmol Playa. Chakalal and Ak 2, single shrines on rocky bays (fig. 14,c), yielded almost no sherds. In 1954 test trenches were also dug at Tulum and Tancah, but in view of the big samples collected from those sites in 1955 the results are not summarized here.

Mulchi

Mulchi is a single-plaza site surrounded by 9 small buildings. The floor of Structure VI, a small east-coast temple, was cleared of debris, and a good sherd sample was collected. In excavating, an altar was uncovered against the back wall. From a field near by a surface collection was also made. The sherd sample breaks down as follows:

Tulum Red	41
Tulum Plain	223
V Fine Orange	15
Mayapan Black-on-cream	11
Chiquila Censer	26
Tulum Buff Paste Censer	7
Tancah Striated	15
Tancah Plain	86 *
Total	424

*Some sherds showing traces of slip may be Tancah Variegated or, more probably, Yucatan Slate.

The Tulum Red sample from Mulchi has a coarser paste than that at Tulum and is brick red; the shapes, however, are typical Tulum Red.

Kilometer 35

Kilometer 35 is very similar to Mulchi in plan and size, but has fewer buildings: 3 platforms surmounted by 5 little temples. The following excavations were conducted.

Trench 1. A floor-clearing operation. Temple 1 is a tiny shrine (fig. 14,d) with a base area only 1.5 by 1.85 m. The roof debris was cleared away, and a small pottery sample was collected from the floor. Thirty sherds, all Tulum Black Paste Censer, including a figurine face, rims, annular base lips, and parts of the feet, arms, and back ornaments of a figurine. Most of them probably come from one or two vessels. In clearing, a small altar was uncovered.

Trench 2. The floor was cleared of debris from Temple 3 (fig. 14,e). Eighty-two sherds of Tulum Black Paste Censer were collected.

Trench 3. A trench dug along the plaza side of the main stairway of the Palace Platform on the east side of the plaza. The platform summit in front of the columns (fig. 14,f) was also cleared, and a series of small, low benches was exposed in front of each column. No arbitrary levels were defined.

From this trench the following wares were recorded:

Tulum Red	20
Tulum Plain	27
Chiquila Censer	22
Tulum Black Paste Censer	19
Total	88

The Tulum Red sherds are of the coarse type noted for Mulchi, and the shapes are not definitive; some may actually be slipped Chiquila Censer ware.

Xelha

Two sherd samples were analyzed from the site of Xelha. One is a large surface collection from a milpa near the plaza; another is from a test trench dug along a house platform in the same field. Trenching around the inside of the plaza failed to reveal good sherd deposits. The break-down by ware of the samples is as follows:

	Surface Collection	Trench
Tulum Red	16	8
Tulum Plain	0	36
Tulum Censer	0	5
Tancah Plain	130	49
Restricted orifice rims	0	14
Yucatan Slate	6	29
Black-on-slate		2
Miscellaneous wares		
Unslipped thick orange	54	0
Totals	206	143

Ak 1

Ak 1 is a small shrine on the shore of a rocky bay. The roof of the structure has collapsed, and only the walls remain (fig. 14,b). The floor was cleared and a small trench dug along the front of the structure. The following sherds were collected:

Tulum Red	5
Chiquila Censer	9
Tulum Buff Paste Censer	1 (almost complete rabbit effigy cup)

Tulum Black Paste Censer	33 (32 plus a shark effigy)
Total	48

Palmol

At Palmol, excavations were confined to the single structure discovered, a two-story temple (fig. 14,g). The stairway of the platform was cleared, and a trench was excavated along the edge of the temple platform from the stairs to the southeast corner. After this another trench was excavated into the platform just east of the stairway. A two-terraced smaller inner platform was uncovered, which probably served as the platform for the earlier inner temple that today is an inner room. Unfortunately no sherds were found in the outer platform fill. Our analyzed sherd sample is from the first trench.

Tulum Red	17
Tulum Buff Paste Censer	32
Tulum Black Paste Censer	2
Tancah Plain	16
Yucatan Slate	1
Total	68

Palmol Playa

This site has two standing structures, a big pyramid and a small flat beam-and-masonry roofed temple (fig. 14,i). The roof has fallen in, but the walls are intact. From a trench excavated along the stairway the following wares were collected:

Tulum Red	7
Chiquila Censer	2 (1 ladle handle)
Tulum Buff Paste Censer	89
Total	98

INTERIOR SITES

Although attention was concentrated mainly on coastal sites a number of interior sites were excavated for ceramic samples: Kantunil Kin, El Diez, Kilometer 14, Leona Vicario, Santa Maria, Solfarino, and Monte Bravo. Good samples were collected at all except Santa Maria and Leona Vicario, which produced little material.

Kantunil Kin

Two excavations were conducted at this site. One was of a small mound in which a series of inner structures was uncovered and trenched. This excavation was summarized in my 1955 report as follows:

"The major excavation at the site was made at one of the small conical mounds about 500 m northeast of the main group. This mound, apparently one of the few not badly destroyed by villagers, was a roughly circular heap of stone about 3 m high. Trenching into the south slope revealed a succession of buried buildings: first a rectangular, three-terraced, white-coated platform; then within this, a single-terraced round platform with a round altar-like elevation on top (fig. 14,k); and finally within this, a smaller, two-terraced round platform (fig. 14,l). Both of the inner round platforms were covered by a coat of black paint. The form of the outermost platform was not determinable but there seems to have been a small stone temple on its summit."

The ware analysis from these levels runs as follows:

	Outer Rubble	Fill of Rectangular Structure	Fill of Outer Round Structure	Fill of Inner Round Structure
Tulum Buff Paste Censer	1	0	0	0
Chiquila Variegated	10	3	1	1
Tancah Plain-Striated	55	7	26	3
Regional Polychrome	22	18	17	3
Totals	88	28	44	7

The Regional Polychrome is all typically Tzakol in form with basal flange bowls and ring bases. The Variegated is very close to that from Chiquila. The Plain ware includes a few striated body sherds, and all but the innermost level yielded reduced orifice bowl rims of the Tancah type. Typical large supports of the Tancah type go with all levels.

A second excavation was conducted along the east side of the west platform on the Main Plaza. The trench, dug at right angles to the mound, measured 1 by 4 m. No great depth of soil was encountered, and no levels were defined. The total sherd count came to 36, which broke down as follows:

Tancah Red	1
Chiquila Variegated	
Buff paste, dark slip	22
Brick paste, cream slip	12
Tancah Plain	1
Total	36

El Diez

At El Diez three small trenches were excavated along the plaza sides of the Main Pyramid (fig. 14,n) and the north and west platforms. A fairly heavy concentration occurred in the trench on the Main Pyramid side, but the total sample was small and was studied as a unit. Ware distribution was as follows:

Tulum Plain	36
V Fine Orange	2
Vista Alegre Striated	44 (10 rims)
Chiquila Variegated	26
Tancah Plain	56 *
Yucatan Slate	24
Miscellaneous, probably burned slate	1 reconstructed vessel plus 26 sherds

*Includes restricted orifice rims and typical hollow supports.

Kilometer 14

A series of small excavations conducted at this site are summarized below.

<u>Trench 1</u>. The small temple on the summit of the Main Pyramid has been almost destroyed by treasure seekers, who broke through the floor and dug into the platform beneath. By culling this throwout a number of sherds were salvaged. Also a small trench was dug at the base of the stairway from which a good ceramic sample was collected.

<u>Trench 2</u>. Another trench was dug along the stairway of Structure 2 (fig. 14,<u>o</u>), the smaller pyramid on top of the huge platform southwest of the Main Pyramid. A small sample was collected.

<u>Trench 3</u>. Trench 3 was dug into the fill of a small platform on the summit of the Great Platform. A fair sample was collected.

The three sherd lots are summarized below:

	Trench 1	Trench 2	Trench 3
Tulum Plain	0	26	0
Chiquila Censer	1 (ladle handle)	22	0
Vista Alegre Striated	8	0	4
Tancah Red	0	0	7
Chiquila Variegated			
Red-on-cream	11	1	0
Other	0	3	3
Tancah Plain	17	16	9
Yucatan Slate	33	0	0
Miscellaneous wares			
Burned slate	26	0	0
Fine paste unslipped *	16	0	0
Coarse paste unslipped †	31	0	0
Totals	143	68	23

*Some sherds have traces of orange slip.

† These are probably Tulum Plain and Tulum Buff Paste Censer, all very small body sherds.

Leona Vicario

Leona Vicario yielded the heaviest proportion of Tancah Red outside of Tancah itself, and the early position of this ware suggests the possibility that the site is one of the earliest in northern Quintana Roo. Unfortunately no really good sherd deposits were found; from several trenches dug around the plaza and a number of house mounds, a total of only 68 sherds was collected, all small and some of dubious identification. The ware breakdown showed Tancah Red 21, Chiquila Variegated 14, Tancah Plain 33.

Santa Maria

Like Leona Vicario, Santa Maria produced very poor samples, and the general size and condition of the sherds make identification difficult. The following types were identified or separated:

Tulum Red	5
Vista Alegre Striated	21

Tancah Red	14
Chiquila Variegated	10
Tancah Plain	42
Miscellaneous, brown slipped fine paste	22
Total	114

Solfarino

A single trench was excavated along the west side of the larger of two little pyramids at this small site. A heavy concentration of pottery was discovered, but in very fragmentary condition. Ware identification of many sherds was impossible.

The sample contained a heavy showing of sherds which in form closely parallel Chiquila Censer ware, including rims and adornos, but they are finer paste and many have a pale pink color rather than the typical brick red of Chiquila Censer, and some even have a buff tint. The sample breaks down as follows:

	Rims	Body Sherds
Pale pink	17	144
Buff	9	27
Brick red	18	145
Smoky	7	35
Totals	51	351

Also in the sample were 1 rim and 17 body sherds of a red slipped ware which could be Tulum Red as far as paste, surface, and slip are concerned. The single rim, however, is a typical Chiquila Censer type, and so we might consider them simply slipped Chiquila Censer of the fine paste variety found at this site and noted above. The remainder of the sample included 1 Regional Polychrome rim, 14 Vista Alegre Striated, and a parrot-head effigy with a brown slip on a fine buff paste ware (fig. 17,t).

Monte Bravo

Two trenches were dug along the bases of the large, low rectangular mounds that make up the site. Samples are large, but sherds are generally very small; only a fraction were classifiable. The results are summarized below:

	Trench 1	Trench 2
Tulum Red (possibly slipped Chiquila Censer)		21
Mayapan Black-on-cream	10	0
Chiquila Censer (red slip)	12	0
Vista Alegre Striated	19	22
Tancah Plain	85	62
Regional Polychrome	35	50
Yucatan Slate	0	9
Miscellaneous, burned slate	41	26
Totals	202	190

5. CHETUMAL AREA

ICHPAATUN

Escalona Ramos (1946) recorded a number of sites from the region around the city of Chetumal. One of them, Ichpaatun, showed striking architectonic similarities to Tulum in the presence of a surrounding wall and columned palaces. His fairly complete description of the site (ibid., pp. 522-30) is summarized below.

Ichpaatun is on the west shore of the Bahia de Chetumal, about 13 km north of the city of Chetumal. Like Tulum the enclosed area is rectangular with the long axis parallel to the beach, and is surrounded by three walls, the east side being delimited by the sea. The north wall measures 300 m, the west 770 m, and the south 400 m. The enclosed space is approximately 27 hectares, or more than twice that of Tulum. Architecturally, however, the site is much less impressive. Only 18 structures were noted by Escalona Ramos, including 2 columned palaces and 16 mounds. The general condition of the structures is very poor. The terrain slopes up abruptly from 100 to 200 m behind the beach and then levels off. Most of the structures are on this elevated plateau-like area, densely clustered around four courts in the center of the long axis of the site.

A stela at the site carries the Long Count date 9.8.0.0.0 5 Ahau 5 Chen.

Four trenches were excavated at Ichpaatun; the results are summarized below:

Trench 1

Trench 1 was excavated along the north edge of the east wing of "El Edificio de las Grandes Columnas" (Structure 1), the larger of the two palaces. It was 3 by 1.5 m in area, and 0.75 m deep to bedrock. As most of the sherds occurred in the first 0.3 m no levels were defined. Sherds were abundant, and the sample further included 1 obsidian core, 7 blades, 1 flint knife, 2 grinding stones, and 1 plastering stone.

Trench 2

Trench 2, 3 m west of the large mound called Structure IV by Escalona Ramos, measuring 2 m square, produced the heaviest ceramic concentration of any single trench in either field season. The total depth was about 1.0 m, and three levels were defined. The lower two levels were later combined, as the yield dropped sharply below 0.3 m and the final level produced a very small sample. Besides sherds the trench also produced the following artifacts:

Level 1: 6 complete spindle whorls and fragments of 5 others, 1 obsidian core, 42 obsidian blades, 1 obsidian scraper, 1 obsidian arrow point, 1 flint scraper, 1 flint lance head, 2 fragments of other flint points.

Level 2: 9 obsidian blades, 1 spindle whorl.

Trench 3

Trench 3, excavated 0.3 m south of Trench 2, was 2 m square. Two levels were defined: 0 to 0.3 m and 0.3 to 0.9 m. Sherd concentration was almost as heavy as in Trench 2; the following artifacts were included:

Level 1: 40 obsidian blades, 1 obsidian core, 1 chert lance point, 3 chert flakes, 9 complete spindle whorls, fragments of 2 other spindle whorls.

Level 2: 8 obsidian blades, 1 chert lance head.

Trench 4

Trench 4, excavated along the east size of El Edificio de Las Pequeñas Columnas south of the stairway, was 2 m wide and 4.5 m long. The face of the platform of the structure is well preserved and rests on bedrock, standing about 0.7 m high. Approximately 0.4 m of soil had accumulated on bedrock, and this was the approximate depth of the trench to the east. Alongside the terrace, however, fallen debris had added another 0.4 m of deposit, almost hiding the terrace face. Most of the sherds came from the soil layer and were abundant, especially plain wares. No levels were defined. In addition to sherds the following artifacts were collected. Obsidian: 1 core, 16 small blades, 1 blade 8 cm long. Chert: 3 flakes. (For illustrations of some of these artifacts see figs. 11,i,2-7; 19,a,3,7-9,11,12; 19,b,3,4.)

Table 3 summarizes the sherd count for post-Classic wares, which make up at least 95 per cent of all samples. The remainder are Classic Period sherds collected in the bottom levels of Trenches 2 and 3.

The table shows little percentile variation in terms of the four basic wares, and in all levels and trenches Tulum Red is the most common, running from 58 to 64 per cent.

Within the evidently short period of occupation at Ichpaatun, although an extremely intensive one, to judge by the size of our samples, some variation is found in the forms of Tulum Red ware. First, within the category of bowls, Trench 2 shows basal flange bowls decreasing markedly from Level 2 to Level 1 and incised and direct rim bowls increasing at an equally well defined rate. Unfortunately Trench 3 does not agree except very unsatisfactorily in the case of the incised and direct rim bowls, and in the basal flange shapes the trend is the reverse. Grater bowls seem to be almost entirely late. Trench 3 in general produced a very poor sample in Level 2 and is probably inferior to Trench 2 for seriation, but even so one hesitates to set up trends when the only deep refuse deposits at Ichpaatun are in disagreement.

In supports, it may be statistically significant that all three of the "Turkish slipper" forms are in the upper levels of the two stratigraphic trenches. Both the conical forms and the only effigy also were from the upper levels.

With respect to jar rims, Trench 2 shows again a much clearer seriation than Trench 3, bolstered rims, rim handles, and incised rims all being restricted to the upper level, and flaring rims being almost three times as common in the bottom levels. The other trench reveals a similar trend, but the statistical differences are slight and could be accidental.

Trench 2 also shows a heavier concentration of Mayapan Black-on-cream in the bottom level than in the upper, but the frequency does not shift significantly in Trench 3.

I suggest very hesitantly that the Ichpaatun samples show a number of possibly significant variations. The following conclusions might be noted.

1. Wares at Ichpaatun are very similar to those at Tulum in paste, surface decoration, and form, indicating a single tradition. On the other hand, Ichpaatun samples of Red ware tend to exhibit more variation in supports, more incision, and generally superior quality in paste and

TABLE 3. FREQUENCIES OF WARES AND SHAPES (POST-CLASSIC) FROM TRENCHES AT ICHPAATUN

	Trench 2		Trench 3		Trench 1	Trench 4	Total
	Level 1	Level 2	Level 1	Level 2			
TULUM RED WARE							
Bowl Forms							
Basal break							
Rims	34	15	20	8	11	10	98
Basal angles	30	0	36	7	11	10	94
Incised rims	2	0	0	0	14	0	16
Basal flanged							
Rims	1	13	9	0	2	2	27
Basal angles	6	14	24	4	2	5	55
Hemispherical							
Direct rims	20	2	19	3	12	0	56
Incised rims	8	1	2	0	4	0	15
Graters	3	1	3	0	0	0	7
Supports							
Turkish slipper	2	0	1	0	0	0	3
Tulum typical	4	3	4	0	12	6	29
Bulbous rattle	3	3	4	3	2 (slit)	0	15
Effigy	1	0	0	0	1	2	4
Small conical	1	0	1	0	0	1	3
Sherds	10	0	21	2	0	12	45
Unclassified rims	46	14	12	0	25	0	97
Unclassified body	120	46	241	16	123	15	561
Unclassified incised	2	0	7	0	23	0	32
Jars							
Rims							
Bolstered	20	0	12	2	2	11	47
Direct	55	19	55	12	9	11	161
Direct incised	6	0	0	0	5	3	14
Direct with rim handles	2	0	3	0	0	2	7
Flaring	20	22	36	8	5	22	113
Flat or concave bases	11	9	41	10	3	17	91
Handles							
Strap	5	9	25	4	9	15	67
Small loop	2	1	1	0	0	1	5
Unclassified shoulder and neck sherds	67	19	94	20	45	65	310
Unclassified body	529	218	702	110	334	513	2406
Unclassified incised	12	12	36	0	15	5	80
Off-color Sherds	183	124	246	57	200	398	1208
Exotic Forms							
Censer types	4	0	4	0	1	0	9
Miniature high-necked forms	0	0	0	0	4	0	4
Step supports	0	0	0	0	1	2	3
Chiquila type rims	0	0	0	0	0	6	6
Unclassifiable Small Rims	0	0	62	12	0	24	98
Coarse Paste	0	0	0	0	26	0	26
Total Tulum Red Ware	1209	545	1721	278	901	1158	5812

(Continued on next page.)

TABLE 3. FREQUENCIES OF WARES AND SHAPES FROM TRENCHES AT ICHPAATUN—Continued

	Trench 2		Trench 3		Trench 1	Trench 4	Total
	Level 1	Level 2	Level 1	Level 2			
TULUM PLAIN WARE							
Bowls and Comals							
Rims	3	2	7	2	43	13	70
Comals	0	0	0	0	18	0	18
Rims with lugs and handles	0	0	1	0	7	2	10
Jars							
Rims	146	86	189	34	102	62	619
Shoulder	31	19	40	7	0	18	115
Bases, flat and concave	4	0	5	0	0	0	9
Handles							
Strap	1	0	2	0	0	0	3
Loop	3	0	2	0	0	0	5
Unclassifiable Body							
(mostly jars)	529	218	702	110	334	513	2406
Total Tulum Plain Ware	717	325	948	153	504	608	3255
MAYAPAN BLACK-ON-CREAM							
Jars							
Rims	12	10	13	7	0	0	42
Neck shoulders	1	4	4	2	0	0	11
Body	9	30	49	3	0	0	91
Strap handles	0	0	4	1	0	0	5
Total Mayapan Black-on-cream	22	44	70	13	0	0	149
ICHPAATUN CENSER WARE							
Rims	7	5	6	3	3	3	27
Pedestal bases	0	0	0	0	3	11	14
Adornos	10	2	8	3	15	11	49
Body	9	14	25	7	16	16	87
Whistles	2	0	3	0	0	0	5
Figurines	0	0	3	1	3	0	7
Ladle							
Handle	0	0	1	1 (effigy)	1	1	4
Bowl rim	1	0	4	0	0	0	5
Total Ichpaatun Censer Ware	29	21	50	15	41	42	198
Tulum Red	1209 (61%)	545 (58%)	1721 (62%)	278 (61%)	901 (62%)	1158 (64%)	5812
Tulum Plain	717 (36%)	325 (35%)	948 (34%)	153 (33%)	504 (35%)	608 (34%)	3255
Mayapan Black-on-cream	22 (1%)	44 (5%)	70 (2%)	13 (3%)	0	0	149
Ichpaatun Censer	29 (1%)	21 (2%)	50 (2%)	15 (3%)	41 (3%)	42 (2%)	198
Grand totals	1977	935	2789	459	1446	1808	9414

surface. The Plain wares also are harder, better fired, and on the whole superior to Tulum Plain and Tulum Buff Paste Censer. Bowls and comals, the former very rare, the latter absent, at Tulum, are common at Ichpaatun.

2. Within the Ichpaatun material some change in rim form may be observed. In Tulum Red, basal flanges tend to be early, hemispherical bowls and graters late, and incision, whether on bowls or jars, increases in frequency. In jar rims, bolstered rims tend to be late and flaring rims early, and Mayapan Black-on-cream tends to be early.

In addition to the Tulum Period assemblage a small sample of Classic pottery occurred in the bottom levels of both Trenches 2 and 3; none was found in Trenches 1 and 4. The total sample breaks down as follows:

Regional Polychrome	6
Yucatan Slate	1
Calderitas Striated	23
Calderitas Red	8
Calderitas Polychrome	3
Total	41

The presence of a small quantity of Classic pottery along with the stela suggests a minor Classic occupation of the site. Theoretically the flat plain below should yield more Classic material, since the stela was found in that area, but no trenches were excavated there.

CALDERITAS

Describing this site, Escalora Ramos (1946, pp. 515) states: "Este núcleo arqueológico se compone de mas de 25 montículos distribuidos alrededor de patios, según un eje general dirigido de N. a S. con una breve desviación de 10° N. al E. El conjunto principal tiene unos 400 m. de largo, según el mismo eje. Un conjunto secundario formado por 3 montículos alrededor de un patio, se halla a otros 400 m. al N. del primero."

Trench 1, 4 by 1.5 m in area, runs along the terrace on the west side of Structure 1. It lies north of the crypt entrance described by Escalona Ramos. Not indicated in his survey is the fact that there is a low apronlike terrace extending west from Structure 1 for 15 m. Trench 1 cuts down into this apron. Two levels were defined. Level 1 is represented by some 0.5 m of top soil that has accumulated on top of the original apron surface. This layer was also filled with fallen masonry debris. Below it there is no floor but a layer of small chunks of limestone 0.25 m thick; below this, 0.5 m of big-stone fill; finally, bedrock. Level 2 includes all sherds from the small-stone or big-stone terrace fill. The following frequency of wares occurred:

	Level 1	Level 2
Classic Wares	(70%)	(100%)
Regional Polychrome	0	1
Yucatan Slate	1	1
Calderitas Striated	180	189
Calderitas Fine Paste Striated	5	0
Calderitas Red	56	175
Calderitas Polychrome	40	65

	Level 1	Level 2
Classic Wares—Continued		
Calderitas Heavy Plain	3	0
Post-Classic Wares	(30%)	0
Tulum Red	28	
Tulum Plain and Eroded Tulum Red	60	
Ichpaatun Censer	35	____
Total	408	431

In our ceramic studies at Tancah we have seen that the Tulum ceramic series is an isolated phenomenon in the charts and rarely occurs mixed with Classic wares. Trench 1 therefore probably represents three phases of occupation at Calderitas. Phase 1 is characterized by a high percentage of both Calderitas Red and Calderitas Striated. Phase 2 would represent the Classic material from the upper level, and here Calderitas Red drops sharply in percentage and Calderitas Striated increases markedly. Furthermore, two new types appear, Fine Paste Striated and Heavy Plain. The final phase presumably represents reuse of the building during the Tulum Period, probably from Ichpaatun, which is only a few kilometers to the north.

Trench 2 was excavated along the west side of Structure 2, a small altar in the center of the Main Plaza. The trench, whose total depth was 1 m, showed the following vertical zoning: (1) upper layer of top soil 0.25 m thick; (2) masonry floor; (3) 0.35-m-thick band of small-stone fill; (4) single layer of bigger stones some 0.2 m thick; and (5) 0.2 m of loose earth, probably the old land surface before the plaza was paved. All the sherds came from the top soil, and almost all are post-Classic in date. They were as follows:

Tulum Red	11
Tulum Plain	54
Ichpaatun Censer	48
Calderitas Striated	10
Calderitas Red	10
Calderitas Polished Black	2
Total	135

Trench 3 was an extensive one running along the west edge of the apronlike extension west of Structure 1. The ancient people evidently swept most of their refuse off the platform into this adjacent area, for sherd refuse was extremely heavy. As the area was in part slump from the adjacent terrace, and debris made up most of the deposit, no levels were defined. The trench attained a total depth of 1 m in spots and covered a total surface area of about 10 sq m. The sample breaks down as follows:

Yucatan Thin Slate	3
Calderitas Striated	637
Calderitas Fine Paste Striated	69
Calderitas Red	245
Calderitas Polychrome	164
Calderitas Polished Black	4
Calderitas Heavy Plain	22
Miscellaneous and tentative	
Plain rims, probably from Calderitas Striated	42
Eroded Calderitas Red	261
Total	1447

6. SETTLEMENT PATTERNS

TANCAH

We have already discussed the operations of trail cutting, mapping, and settlement-pattern trenching at Tancah. In this section we will consider the results of these techniques and assess the settlement pattern of the site.

Building Remains. Groups A and B are, with very little doubt, entirely religious in function; none of the structures could have served even as a priestly dormitory. Our map (fig. 1) is complete except for a few structures to the west and northwest, of which there are 15 at most, to judge from our western extensions of grid trails. Furthermore, this area is mostly open pasture so that observation was relatively easy.

The 46 newly mapped structures may be summarized in the following list.

Large platforms without masonry structures	8
Large platforms with masonry temples on summits	3
Medium-sized platforms	5
Small platforms	8
Altars	4
Masonry temples	4
Pyramids	1
Dry stone walls	8
Retaining walls of terraces	5

Under the category of large platforms are 8 that do not have religious structures of masonry on their summits. They are huge low platforms; 3 of them have simple rectangular ground plans, and the others have inset or stepped plans. They run approximately 1 m in height, and they have an outside shell of roughly cut stone blocks with a rubble fill. They are from 30 to 60 m long and from 15 to 40 m wide. Their large size indicates that they were the bases for perishable structures used as either elite residences or more probably as priests' dormitories. Outside the carefully mapped area north of Structure 60 is another huge platform of this type.

When I first noted the 3 huge platforms with masonry temples of the typical east-coast diminutive size on their summits, I thought that they might be an example of Tulum Period building on old abandoned residential platforms of the Tancah Period, but, unfortunately for that conclusion, the style fits in neatly with the other structures at Tancah, 2 of them, for instance, having three-member moldings which are lacking at Tulum but are characteristic of Tancah architecture. They seem to have been built as temple platforms.

Most of the medium-sized platforms are rectangular in ground plan; a few are square, and one is L-shaped. In basal area they run around 200 to 300 sq m, and they could have supported substantial-sized houses. There were 5 of them in the mapped area and approximately 5 more just west of the end of our formal grid pattern but within the area reached by the western trail extensions, making 10 in all.

Small platforms numbered 8 within our site plan, but at least 7 more lie northwest and west of our surveyed area. I suspect that the total number of structures of this type at Tancah within the area defined as the site may run as high as 20 but not more. They too could have served as bases for small houses of the size found in modern Yucatecan villages. Extending westward from the area defined as the site of Tancah are numerous clusters of some 6 to 12 small platforms, along with 1 or 2 medium-sized platforms and a small pyramid, each cluster forming a distinct group, perhaps hamlet-type settlements dependent on Tancah. Time did not permit either mapping of these small clusters or trenching for dating. Some of them probably date from the Tulum Period and were dependent on Tulum rather than on Tancah.

The single pyramid among the new structures along with another in the unmapped area west of the gridded zone are typical pyramidal structures which probably supported temples of perishable materials on their summits.

Of interest are the extensive low, dry stone walls similar in construction to the house-lot walls from Mayapan. They occur at Tancah in connection with the larger structures. The 2 most clearly defined, Structures 29 and 41-53, are obviously related to ceremonial structures (the former to Group A; the second connects Group B with the masonry structures on top of Platforms 51 and 42). House-lot walls like those at Mayapan are lacking. In construction and function these walls at Tancah resemble those around the main plaza at Aguada Grande on Cozumel Island described in my 1955 report.

In summary, we find at Tancah the following structures which may have served as residential platforms: (1) 9 large platforms, possibly priests' dormitories or elite residences; (2) 10 medium-sized platforms which could have served as platforms for rather large houses; (3) at least 15, possibly as many as 20, platforms that could have supported individual family houses like those used today in Yucatecan villages.

Even if we assume all these structures to have been inhabited simultaneously the total population at Tancah could not have numbered more than a few hundred inhabitants, including priests and proletariat. (I suspect that the smaller structures were residences for full-time craftsmen.) These structures are scattered over an area measuring 480 by 420 m, or approximately 20 hectares.

Occupational Debris. The main purpose of the settlement-pattern trenching was to assess the gross intensity of occupation on the basis of sherd counts, and with this statistical tool to obtain at least a subjective impression of site demography and to ascertain whether there was a densely congested urban population besides that residing in structures built on the summits of stone platforms. The results were of great interest, and they present, I believe, a good impression of the character of Maya use of these major centers.

The accompanying map (fig. 1) illustrates the situation. On the map the settlement-pattern trenches are divided into four classes based on total sherd counts for each trench. These classes, which are shown by different symbols, are: (1) below 25 sherds; (2) 25 to 50 sherds; (3) 50 to 100 sherds; and finally (4) more than 100 sherds. It must be emphasized here that all sherds were counted, regardless of size, and that most were so small as to be unclassifiable with regard to our types. Often only one-third of the total sherds collected could be classified, and never more than two-thirds. Moreover, it must be pointed out that these sherd concentrations represent some 1000 years of almost continuous occupation plus a reuse of the area for a century or two during the Tulum Period. Soil deposition over the site is relatively heavy for Yucatan, with numerous trenches running below 0.5 m depth, so that lack of soil and therefore erosion of surface sherds is not a factor at Tancah. Of interest is the sparse concentration of cultural debris over the site as a whole. Of the 184 trenches, 103 yielded less than 25 sherds each, 136 yielded less than 50 each, and only 17 yielded more than 100. With respect to the precise distribution of heavy and light deposits the following conclusions may be drawn.

(a) The system employed is very useful in setting up the absolute limits of a Maya center. Grid Line 1 limits the site to the east with but one of the trenches yielding over 25 sherds, and Grid Line 16 running at right angles to and east of this trail with three trenches did not yield a single sherd. The southern limits of the site as far as refuse concentrations are concerned lie within 100 m of Group A and 40 m of Group B. To the north the heavy deposits end but 80 m from the north edge of Group A. Grid-line extensions north and south of these points revealed in many trenches a complete absence of sherds, in others less than 10. To the west the site was not delimited by the survey, but it probably does not extend more than 50 m west of our grid-line extensions and may be much less as there are few structures in that area. Except to the east, where the terrain drops off sharply to the coastal swamp, there are no ecological reasons for these sharply defined limits. The area of fair to heavy ceramic deposits, then, is limited to a long, narrow rectangle measuring 280 m north-south and about 480 m east-west.

(b) Within this area of sherd concentration the distribution is very uneven and with few exceptions is related to the position of the described architectonic features. In a large area between Group A and Structures 42 and 51 some 43 trenches were excavated, of which only 4 yielded more than 25 sherds. This area is also bare of architectural features except for Group B itself. Of the 17 trenches that yielded an excess of 100 sherds, 11 form a ring around Group A and obviously represent rubbish deposits from the use of the religious precinct rather than occupational debris (unless it could be believed that the surrounding population used the outskirts of the plaza as a town dump!). Four others lie off the edges of large platforms in the western edge of the site. Of the 31 trenches yielding between 50 and 100 sherds, 11 were along the edges of Group A, 12 off big platforms in the northwest quadrant of the site, and 2 near large structures in the southwest segment of the zone. Some of the remainder are related to other isolated structures.

(c) Not all the area of heavy sherd concentration was occupied simultaneously. Our sherd frequencies show a significant sorting-out by period from east to west. A small rectangle measuring 220 by 100 m, including in it Group A, was evidently the Late Formative-Early Classic center and was not utilized during the Late Classic Period for either ritual or occupational purposes. A new ceremonial zone, Group B plus the big platforms with summit temples, was constructed and a new habitation area set aside.

Most of the area south of the Plaza of Group A, which includes most of the rectangle of Late Formative-Early Classic occupation, shows clear evidence that it is a built-up zone. Most of the trenches reveal heavy concentrations of limestone fragments, and the terrain slopes down sharply both east and west. The area is probably the eroded remains of an extensive terrace running south from Group A. If so, the sherd material excavated may well be fill brought from surrounding hamlets and therefore not represent primary occupational debris. In its Early Classic occupation the area may have been a ceremonial center of the Classic type with next to no resident population.

The rest of the site shows a definite correlation between deep deposits with fair to heavy sherd samples and the platforms of varying sizes. The sherd frequencies consistently suggest a Middle to Late Classic Period dating, and we might visualize the Late Classic Period utilization of the site as including a ceremonial precinct to the south taking in Group B and Structures 42 and 51 with their small summit temples. The intervening space between these two ceremonial complexes was evidently occupied by a big, open plaza limited north and south by low, dry stone walls. To the west and north of the plaza was the elite residential district with numerous platforms of various sizes ranged in courts or isolated. That the orientation of these structures seems not to have been co-ordinated also suggests their use as residences. This area of heavy settlement covered some 6 hectares, which with the ceremonial zone to the south indicates a total site area for the period of perhaps 9 to 10 hectares. The population probably included priests and a few craftsmen for temple maintenance, but there was no industrial proletariat at any period of occupation at Tancah.

(d) The settlement pattern at Tancah differs markedly from that of modern Yucatecan communities, especially in a feature I am calling "top-heaviness," which seems to be characteristic of ancient Maya centers. By this word I mean that the religious or ceremonial center is extensive in relation to the occupation zone, as compared with highland Mesoamerican sites. In functional terms we have a ceremonial zone without the outlying industrial wards of highland centers. In modern Yucatan a civic center of the size and complexity represented by Tancah would have a community of at least 2000 to 3000 people and a settlement zoning extending at least 2 km from the center in all directions. If, from a modern town like Izamal, all the thatch and wattle houses were removed, leaving just the plaza and masonry houses within a block of the plaza (the houses of the Gente de Vestido), the settlement pattern at Tancah would be reproduced. The rest of the population instead of being nucleated as in modern communities would be scattered in the small hamlet communities represented by the smaller house-mound groups west of Tancah.

TULUM

<u>Building Remains</u>. The settlement pattern at Tulum exhibits certain marked differences from that at Tancah. First, and highly significant in terms of the sociopolitical implications, is the presence of a surrounding wall. Tulum has an artificial delimitation that Tancah lacks, and this simplifies at least one of our settlement-pattern problems, the absolute limits of a "site." Second, in sharp distinction to Tancah, Tulum gives the impression of having a master plan. The Main Street axis suggests town planning, and almost all buildings at Tulum, both civic and residential, are oriented on a single axis. Third, residential structures of stone of the palace type are found at Tulum, in marked contrast to Tancah, where all the masonry structures are religious in function. Finally, as our ceramic data prove, Tulum was a center that was occupied but a fraction of the time that Tancah was in use, certainly not more than one-fifth of the time span and possibly as little as one-tenth. Tancah is a typical Maya Classic center with its separate clusters or groups representing separate construction projects; the only major lack at Tancah is the characteristic causeway system connecting groups. Tulum is a typical highland center with its over-all planning and orientation of the architecture.

In an earlier section we briefly outlined the major subareas at Tulum, and these will form the basis of our discussion.

Our survey and surface observations show conclusively that the space enclosed by the Great Wall is the settlement area of the site. It covers some 7 hectares, or about one-third the area of Tancah. Tulum, then, in terms of its formal architecture, is more nucleated or concentrated than Tancah, although having almost the same number of stone structures if the low corral-like stone walls and terrace facings at Tancah are excluded.

The structures of the Inner Enclosure seem to have served entirely religious functions. The Castillo is quite obviously the principal temple, and I suspect that the priests serving it resided in rooms <u>c</u>, <u>d</u>, <u>e</u>, and <u>f</u> (see Lothrop, 1924, fig. 41), which represent an earlier palace-like structure. Structure 10, called by Lothrop a palace, quite probably served religious functions also.

Structures 45-54 and 35 undoubtedly were small temples, the last possibly linked to the Chac cult with its architectural affiliation with the cenote.

Of great significance is the fact that all structures but one (16) lying along Main Street seem to have been residential. The Structures 21-25 Group forms a unit and conceivably was the residence of the local cacique. Structures 20 and 34 might be interpreted as residences of lesser officials, possibly, in view of the militaristic pattern of late Yucatecan culture, heads of warrior orders. Some writers have argued against calling such structures palaces, because of the shrine and altar centrally located in the same manner as in the temples. Actually this argument is weak, since such writers as Sahagun point out the presence of household shrines and altars in rulers' and nobles' residences in the Valley of Mexico.

The entire Northeast Quadrant of the site seems not to have been used for residence except possibly the flat plain north of Structure 25 which we tentatively identified as a "market." Refuse here is very heavy, and the plain may well have been an area of nucleated population. At any rate it is small, not larger than a third of a hectare.

One of the places of most intensive occupation at Tulum seems to have been the Northwest Quadrant, or that area lying between Main Street and the West Wall and north of the West Gateway in the Great Wall; it measures 1.1 hectares. Almost the entire west edge of Main Street here is lined by a series of platforms which together form a nearly continuous retaining wall. Each is clearly defined, however, has its own stairway, and presumably represents a separate house. These platforms include Structures 19, 26, 27, 28, 29, 30, 31, and 32. Very likely they had pole-and-thatch dwellings on top. Lothrop's map does not show a stairway for Structure 30, but later work, done by the Instituto Nacional, has disclosed one. Trenching revealed the west edges of two of these platforms, and so I was able to estimate their floor-plan area. Structure 29, for example, is 13 m north-south along Main Street and runs westward 15 m. Structure 30, shown by Lothrop as a very extensive single platform, is really several; one measures 8 m along Main Street and runs westward 9 m. Between Structures 30 and 31 is a 50-m gap with no retaining wall along the street; ceramic refuse here is heavy, and I suspect that there once were platform retaining walls along the gap. Structure 32 measures 10 m north-south by 11 m east-west.

If the supposition about the present breaks in the retaining wall is correct, we might picture Main Street, at the time of its use as a thoroughfare, as completely lined with pole-and-thatch structures, almost wall to wall and about the size of modern houses in Yucatan, all the way from Structures 20 to 32. On the basis of the average width of the platforms preserved we might postulate that some 12 houses fronted on Main Street. The ceramic refuse deposits confirm this reconstruction conclusively. Main Street has a deeper soil deposit than any other area of the site except the "Market," and sherd concentrations are relatively heavy; evidently the residents of the houses tossed their garbage into the street. The only Main Street trench that did not yield over 25 sherds was along the edge of Structure 29, and here excavation was suspended on account of the presence of a large number of big fragments of limestone, evidently slump from the terrace fill, which made digging almost impossible.

Occupational Debris. Checking over the sherd samples from the settlement-pattern trenches behind these platforms in the Northwest Quadrant reveals some interesting possibilities. Four grid lines were run from Main Street to the West Wall. The location of the grid lines and the trenches along them is shown on the map (fig. 2); results of the digging and certain other details are shown in table 4.

Although the interpretation of the sherd samples from the Northwest Quadrant presents a number of problems, certain general conclusions can be drawn. Erosion has undoubtedly affected the distribution of material somewhat, but a fairly even belt of heavy sherd deposition runs parallel to Main Street about 10 to 30 m back from it. Grid Line 2 revealed a terrace face in very poor condition about 27 m back of Main Street (fig. 3,g), and the ends of the Main Street platforms range between 11 and 13 m from it. The almost destroyed terrace along with the sherd distribution suggests (and I wish to emphasize the word suggests) the presence of a second parallel line of houses similar to that along Main Street with a street about 12 m wide separating them.

TABLE 4. SETTLEMENT-PATTERN TRENCHES AT TULUM

(All trenches 1 by 1 m unless otherwise noted)

Grid Line	Trench	Sherds	Depth Soil (cm)	Remarks
1	1	6	10	On Main Street along Str. 29; 1- by 4-m trench; soil mixed with stone.
	2	17	5-35	On west edge of Str. 29; mixed earth and stone.
	3	325	30-40	At base of abrupt slope; possibly sherd concentration due to erosion; trench 2 by 2 m.
	4	70	40	On slope.
	5	30	25	On top of ridge.
	6	25	30	Against West Wall.
2	7	35	50	On Main Street alongside Str. 30; 1 flint knife.
	8	11	40	West edge of Str. 30.
	9	70	30	At base of abrupt slope; sherd concentration possibly due to erosion.
	10	20	50	On top of terrace with retaining wall.
	11	24	25	On top of ridge.
	12	0	0	4 m from West Wall; surface bedrock.
3	13	53	40	On Main Street.
	14	70	50	On flat level surface.
	15	36	30	Gentle slope; 3 fragments of metate.
	16	0	20	Big stones mixed with earth; probably terrace fill.
	17	3	5	On top of ridge; surface bedrock.
	18	44	30	4 m from Great Wall; mainly surface bedrock.
4	19	90	30	On Main Street alongside Str. 32.
	20	141	50-70	West edge of Str. 32.
	21	31	40	On flat level surface.
	22	28	40	Gradual slope.
	23	5	30	Gradual slope.
	24	2	0	2 m from West Wall; no soil; surface bedrock.
5				Base line along Main Street.
6	25	21	20 soil 30 stone fill	Layer of soil, then terrace fill; flat surface.
	26	18	15-40	Level surface.
	27	25	30	On very gentle slope.
	28	0	0	Surface bedrock.
	29	0	0	Surface bedrock; 2 m from West Wall.
7	30	32	30-60	Mixed soil and stone; flat surface.
	31	51	25-35	Mixed soil and stone; flat surface.
	32	9	10-20	Gentle slope.
	33	0	5	Gentle slope; 6 m from West Wall.
8 west side	34	18	40	Mixed soil and stone; flat surface.
	35	20	40	Very gradual slope.
	36	2	5	Very gradual slope.
	37	6	10-15	Very gradual slope; 4 m from West Wall.
8 east side	38	14	40	Mixed soil and stone; flat surface.
	39	40	50	Mixed soil and stone; flat surface.
	40	51	50	Mixed soil and stone.
	41	41	60	Mixed soil and stone; sloping terrain; in front of Terrace 1.
	42	17	25-30	Mixed soil and stone; sloping terrain; on top of Terrace 1.
	43	33	20	At west edge of Terrace 2.
	44	57	30	On top of Terrace 2.

(Continued on next page)

TABLE 4. SETTLEMENT-PATTERN TRENCHES AT TULUM—Continued

(All trenches 1 by 1 m unless otherwise noted)

Grid Line	Trench	Sherds	Depth Soil (cm)	Remarks
8 east side—Continued				
	45	63	.20	On top of Terrace 3; east edge of Str. 51.
	46	61	50-60	On top of sea cliff ridge; flat terrain.
	47	38	5	On top of sea cliff ridge 8 m from edge; flat terrain.
9 west side	48	22	30	Flat terrain along Main Street.
	49	0	5	Very gentle slope.
	50	10	15-30	Very gentle slope.
	51	0	5-10	Very gentle slope; 8 m from West Wall.
9 east side	52	11	10-15	Flat surface east of Main Street; soil and stone.
	53	1	20-25	Flat surface east of Main Street; soil mixed with stone.
	54	60	60-70	Base of sharp slope; mixed soil and stone.
	55	36	50	On sharply sloping terrain; mixed soil and stone.
	56	32	50	West of Terrace 1 wall; sharp slope; mixed soil and stone.
	57	9	20	West of Terrace 2; sharp slope; mixed earth and stone.
	58	85	80-90	On top of Terrace 2; mixed soil and stone; flat surface.
	59	59	30	On top of Terrace 3; on Str. 60.
	60	10	0	Sunken court between two platforms; surface bedrock.
	61	0	5	East of sunken court.
	62	13	5-10	On top of sea cliff ridge; along east edge of platform.
10 west side	63	8	40-50	Flat surface.
	64	28	35	Flat surface.
	65	12	5	Flat surface.
	66	0	0	Flat surface.
10 east side	67	4	25	Very gentle slope.
	68	25	20	Very gentle slope.
	69	3	10-25	Very gentle slope.
	70	31	25-35	In front of Terrace 1; gradually sloping surface.
	71	?	20-30	On top of Terrace 1; gradually sloping surface.
	72	7	15	On top of Terrace 2 and on Str. 50; gradually sloping surface.
	73	3	0-10	Rounded knoll; very little soil.
	74	23	20-30	Rounded knoll; very little soil.
	75	7	15	Rounded knoll; very little soil.
	76	5	20	Rounded knoll; very little soil.
	77	23	30	Rounded knoll; very little soil.

We might estimate the total number of houses in this area, then, as about 24. The space back of Structures 20-19 may also have had a few houses, but the presence of the West Gateway at this point suggests that the area was probably kept open as an entrance avenue to Main Street and the Inner Enclosure. The central third of the site, aside from the big palaces, probably was not residential.

On purely logical grounds the southern third of the walled area presents the most obvious possibility of residential use, since civic buildings are almost nonexistent. Five grid lines were cut east-west across this part of the site running at right angles to Main Street. The location of the grid lines and the trenches is shown on the map (fig. 2), and other information is in table 4.

The distance from the sea cliff to the West Wall is approximately 150 to 170 m. From the West Wall to a point 100 m east, and including Main Street (fig. 3,g), the terrain is almost flat. The street here lacks retaining walls and cannot be clearly delimited. The remainder of the distance is a sharply sloping incline for some 40 to 50 m, leveling off for the final 20 m or so of flat-topped ridge before dropping sheer to the beach below. The exact point of the start of slope and leveling off varies from one place to another, but the general outlines are consistent.

In the flat area west of Main Street sherd deposits are scanty. In 21 trenches excavated in this area only 3 yielded more than 25 sherds, and 11 yielded fewer than 10. The evidence indicates that the area was but lightly used for habitations. The same holds to a lesser degree for the flat area east of Main Street. Trenches suggested that some artificial leveling was also done here, since the soil is full of loose rock in contrast to the area west of the street. Presumably the sherds represent erosion from the slope to the east or simply a use of the flat area off Main Street as a town dump.

The sloping terrain to the east of Main Street has abundant structural evidence of occupation. Lothrop in his map of Tulum showed at least 3 house terraces on the slope and 4 more on the ridge just west and north of Structure 54. Vertical sections were made of Grid Lines 8 and 9 (fig. 3,g), on the basis of which I postulate at least 3 main tiers of terraces including the ridge top. And there may have been 2 tiers on top of the ridge, bringing the total to 4. Structures 46-47 and 48 belong to the lowest terrace; 52-53-51 belong to the final or ridge-top series. Lothrop mapped only one structure on the middle tier, Structure 50.

The total area covered by these terrace dwellings is approximately 1.2 hectares. Here the housing was evidently more congested, as the terraces are narrow and directly succeed one another, without a broad intervening street as in the Northwest Quadrant. On the basis of the length of these tiers, and of platform size at Tulum as a whole, we might make an outside estimate of some 30 houses for the area, assuming 3 tiers of houses, or 40 houses assuming 4 tiers.

The habitations we have been analyzing for the southern and northwestern parts of the site are in general about the size of those in modern Yucatecan communities and presumably represent working-class or possibly military-class residences. In the two urbanized zones we find a postulated 54 to 64 houses clustered in 2.3 hectares of space. Even if we assume other houses of this type scattered through the remaining areas of the site the total cannot have exceeded about 70 to 80. If we assume them to have been occupied simultaneously we can calculate a total population of perhaps 350 to 400 people. At Tulum the possibilities are greater than at Tancah for simultaneous use of all house structures because of the shorter time range of the site. Add to this the priestly and palace personnel and we might estimate a grand total of 500 to 600 permanent inhabitants for Tulum at its maximum prosperity, in other words a small urban town with perhaps double the resident population of Tancah in one-third the space. In terms of community density we have an over-all figure of 7000 to 8800 persons per square kilometer, which is almost exactly that of a modern town in the Valley of Mexico.

The most interesting feature about our comparison of Maya Classic and Mexican Period settlement patterns lies in the gross population of these major east-coast centers. What seems to have happened historically is an attempt by migrating highland groups at a more congested nucleated settlement, of the highland town type, in an area unsuited for it. The result was an achievement of nucleation but without any great increase in the size of the population; the people were simply concentrated in a smaller area, which was walled in as a military defense measure. The increased population density of the community may, indeed, be related to the problem of defense—the more compact a community the easier it is to fortify—a fact that originally may have been one of the reasons for the rise of the true town and true village in highland Mesoamerica. The limitation of gross size in urban population in Yucatan must surely be related to the differing efficiency of the irrigation-calmil-tlacolol agricultural system of the highlands and the slash-and-burn system of the east coast. Mayapan was much larger than Tulum, but the greater size was made possible only by the forceful establishment of hegemony over a huge area and force feeding of the center by a permanent imported highland militocracy. Actually Landa's data suggest that Mayapan's population consisted largely of subject-town chiefs and their entourages, who may not have lived all year round at the center (Tozzer, 1941, pp. 25-26).

The over-all density of ceramic remains at Tulum confirms my estimate of the more congested pattern. The table compares the settlement-pattern trenches of Tulum with those of Tancah:

	Tulum	Tancah
Below 25 sherds	43	103
25-50 sherds	19	33
50-100 sherds	13	31
Over 100 sherds	2	17
Total	77	184

On first sight there seems to be little if any difference, and significantly more deep deposits occurred at Tancah than Tulum. It must be pointed out, however, that trenches at Tulum are 1 by 1 m in area, at Tancah 1 by 1.5 m, and so our Tulum sherd counts should be corrected upward 50 per cent. Moreover, most of the settlement-pattern trenches at Tancah with heavy yields are off Plaza A and other big structures; at Tulum none of them are, and our stratigraphic trenches dug off the main buildings (both palaces and temples) yielded much more heavily than those in connection with major structures at Tancah. Finally, the Tulum sherd concentrations represent only one or two centuries of accumulation, those from Tancah at least five times that long. With respect to the last point it is of interest to note that, in general, post-Classic centers in Quintana Roo have much more refuse in and around the temples than Classic sites. This finding seems to reflect a more constant use of such structures and implies a larger resident population. If we were to calculate the production per cubic volume of soil, the more intensive occupation at Tulum would become clear, since soil deposition is much heavier at Tancah than at Tulum (at least twice as deep on the average) and the sherds are scattered through a much greater depth. The table showing soil depth at the two sites makes this clear:

NUMBER OF TRENCHES AT TANCAH AND TULUM ACCORDING TO DEPTH

Depth (cm)	0-10	11-20	21-30	31-40	41-50	51-60	61-70	71-80	81-90	91-100	Over 100
Tancah	12	15	8	17	20	15	16	24	13	5	33
Tulum	17	13	23	11	8	3	1		1		

Along with the important quantitative differences in settlement patterns between Tancah and Tulum are striking contrasts in the character of the community as well. The building of stone palaces at Tulum indicates a rising political caste and a lesser importance of the theocracy in social ordering than at Tancah. The city wall suggests a much more aggressive competitive social atmosphere. The proletariat was apparently much larger at Tulum than at Tancah, and the gross difference in site population is mostly due to the increase in this group. The strict ordering of this population in space, with regular streets, is a pale reflection of highland Mesoamerican cultural patterns in which the major interest, evidently from Classic times on, was the organization of people rather than the development of science and art. In short, Tulum and Tancah exemplify the basic cultural difference between the Maya and the Toltec-Aztec.

One of the puzzling problems at Tulum is the function of the walled area just south of and adjacent to the Main Enclosure. Six trails were cut at intervals in this area, which was mostly low scrub, to facilitate surface observation. Only on the ridge adjacent to the Great Wall (the South Wall of the Main Enclosure) were found signs of occupation, in the form of a few platforms and sherd deposits. Most of the area is flat, level terrain with almost no soil and little evidence of ceramic remains. Its function could be interpreted in two ways: as a refuge fort for the surrounding population scattered in hamlets, or as a new settlement project that never materialized.

MISCELLANEOUS SITE PATTERNS

Although the primary objective of the 1954 field season was the collection of sherd samples for chronological analysis, and the gross mapping of sites, considerable amounts of data were also collected on settlement patterns. These data are not conclusive, of course; the longest period spent at a single site was one week, and most sites were visited for only two or three days. For very small ones this length of time was ample for classification of types of site, but for the larger ones it certainly was insufficient.

Techniques consisted of careful searching in milpas adjacent to sites for surface cultural debris (sherds, stone implements, etc.) and for house platforms, and cutting of trails through the forest tangent to the ceremonial complexes. Secondary indications of the density of population at a center might be estimated on the basis of pottery concentrations in test excavations, although the majority of the excavations were made within the ceremonial complexes.

Five basic types of site seem to occur in Quintana Roo.

First, and most common, is what we might call the Tancah Settlement Pattern type, after the site for which we have most complete data. In this type one or more ceremonial plazas is surrounded by religious buildings, mainly temples, with scattered individual religious structures or small groups at some distance from the main center. In major centers these outlying units form groups or clusters; in smaller ones they are more likely to be detached individual temples and pyramids. Along with these religious buildings are a limited number of what are probably platforms for pole-and-thatch residences. In Quintana Roo they are usually large structures and very limited in number, but there is considerable variation in the degree of concentration and in the total number of these structures. In an intensive wandering around Kantunil Kin over a two-week stay very few house platforms were observed. Tancah, which is smaller than Kantunil, has many more. In general, coastal sites show more evidence of occupation, both in architectonic evidence and in surface indications of habitation refuse; and post-Classic sites show more than Classic. Also sites with Late Classic occupation show more refuse than Early Classic. Some coastal sites of this type, such as Cancun and Vista Alegre, were fairly densely clustered. In spite of the over-all variation, however, we do not find large populations nucleated at any site of this class, and the over-all size of the platforms indicates a few well-to-do families in full-time residence and little if any industrialization. If some of the coastal centers were small merchant communities, the more abundant evidence of population concentration would be explained, but even so the assemblages were small, not true towns or cities. Sites of this category include Kantunil Kin, Kilometer 14, El Diez, Santa Maria, Leona Vicario, Solfarino, Chiquila, Vista Alegre, Cancun, El Meco, Mulchi, Kilometer 35, Tancah, Xelha, Palmol, and San Gervasio.

The second type of site consists of an isolated shrine, including one or two temples or a temple and a dormitory, situated within a few hundred meters of the beach or on rocky headlands or shores of bays overlooking the sea. Probably the shrines were for traveling merchants or fishermen, and they are very numerous in the Territory. Sites falling in this category include

Ak 1, Ak 2, Chakalal, Palmol Playa, Cocal 1 and 2, Celerain 1 and 2, Punta Islote, El Real, Arrecife site, Mujeres Island, and Janan.

The third type, possibly the most common of all, is the farming hamlet. Unfortunately time did not permit survey or mapping of a single one of these extremely important settlement types. Extending inland from Tancah for at least 2 km are a large number of these small sites, each including a half dozen to a dozen house platforms, often associated with a single small pyramid. They undoubtedly represent small hamlets of farmers, and there are thousands of them in the Territory. Gaspar Antonio Xiu states in the Relación de Mérida (Relaciones de Yucatán, 1:37-75) that this was the typical lower-class mode of settlement in northern Yucatan.

The fourth, a very rare settlement type, is what we can call the Tulum type. These settlements are entirely post-Classic in date and are characterized by residential palaces of stone, more nucleated populations, and relatively abundant indications of habitation, and they are surrounded by fortified walls. Mayapan and Tulum are classic examples, and Xkaret and Ichpaatun may also be of this type; the only problem with respect to the latter two is whether there was a nucleated population or not. In spite of the greater intensification of settlement, however, the total population of the community remained small, probably because of the difficulty of producing and transporting food with slash-and-burn agriculture in such an unfavorable ecological setting as northern Quintana Roo.

The fifth and final type is a rare (one example) and fascinating one which I noted at Aguada Grande on Cozumel Island. The site has been described in my 1955 report in some detail. It consists of a small ceremonial center which has buildings (small shrines) on two sides and a dry stone wall on the other two. The surrounding bush is divided by these low, dry stone walls into house lots, in each of which is a house platform. Both the house platforms and the lots present a great range of sizes. The lots, in general, form irregular squares or rectangles, in over-all pattern and size closely resembling a modern Yucatecan village, and the question arises as to the possibility of the site's being mostly post-Conquest. The ceramic material suggests precisely this. Arguing against the possibility, however, is the fact that house-lot walls do occur at Mayapan, although they lack the regularity of the Aguada Grande ones.

7. CHRONOLOGY IN QUINTANA ROO

TULUM - TANCAH AREA

In this discussion we shall emphasize the small area around Tulum and Tancah, where we have our longest chronology that is also backed by our most intensive field work with our largest samples.

Tulum and Tancah are situated only a few kilometers apart, and Lothrop (1924) in his monumental study noted the sharp divergences within the general east-coast architectural style between the two sites. He saw them as chronologically important distinctions, and dated Tancah early in his east-coast sequence. Our field survey confirmed this, but Tancah turned out to be much earlier than he anticipated.

In the small area intensively worked, Tancah and Tulum, three obvious and clear-cut ceramic assemblages are apparent. All three occur at Tancah, the final one, however, being the result of a minor reuse of abandoned buildings. We might refer to the earlier assemblages as Group A and Group B complexes, although the extremely small size of our samples from Group B may perhaps be misleading. The Group A ceramic complex includes as diagnostic wares Tancah Red and Tancah Variegated with Tancah Plain and Striated as constant unslipped wares. The Group B complex includes Yucatan Medium Slate and Thin Slate and a strong consistent secondary concentration of Regional Polychrome which first appears in the Group A complex toward the end of the main occupation. These two major chronological divisions seem certain, and what stratigraphic evidence we have from Tancah indicates that A is earlier. The intensive occupation at Tancah, then, can be defined in two major phases. In our section on Tancah ceramic chronology we have suggested a breakdown of the earlier period into two, possibly three, phases, inasmuch as in the earliest levels Tancah Red seems to be more abundant than Variegated, in the middle levels Variegated is more abundant, and in the final levels slipped ware in general declines as compared with Plain ware and Regional Polychrome appears for the first time. I must emphasize here that our samples are small and that this chronological breakdown is only tentatively suggested.

The third ceramic complex represented in our area may be called the Tulum complex. This is again sharply and clearly distinguishable from the other two and appears at Tancah as a post-abandonment, truncated seriation level. It includes such wares as Tulum Red, Tulum Plain, Tulum Buff Paste Censer, Mayapan Black-on-cream, V Fine Orange, and in the final phase Tulum Black Paste Censer.

Tulum seems to fit entirely within this ceramic assemblage. Our extensive excavation survey of that site did not reveal a single sherd from the Tancah Group A or Group B complex. Also we were unable to break down the Tulum complex into phases, with one exception. This exception was probably a post-occupational use of the site after the population either had disappeared or had sharply decreased, and is defined by the above-floor deposits of Tulum Black Paste Censer.

We then have for the Tulum-Tancah area the following chronological divisions:

Group A Complex. Tancah Red, Variegated, Plain, Striated.
        Phases: A. Predominance of Red over Variegated.
                  B. Predominance of Variegated over Red.
                  C. Predominance of plain over slipped wares; appearance of Regional
                     Polychrome.

Group B Complex. Yucatan Medium Slate, Yucatan Thin Slate, Regional Polychrome, Tancah Plain wares with one new form—restricted orifice bowls.

Tulum Complex. Tulum Red, Buff Paste Censer, Plain, V Fine Orange, Mayapan Black-on-cream.
Phases: A. Main period of occupation.
              B. Continued use after abandonment of center—Tulum Black Paste Censer.

Present at Tancah mixed with our Group B complex are a few sherds of Vista Alegre Striated, a ware that presents one of the knottiest chronological problems in our survey. Its position will be discussed shortly.

My limited survey accompanied by small-scale sampling of some 40 sites spread over the northern third of the Territory has previously been mentioned. The restricted number of site samples, the huge geographical range, and the small size of many of the samples make analysis and conclusions difficult and rather precarious, but certain recurrent, consistent patterns may be observed, and they seem to fit our better-documented data from Tulum and Tancah. I wish to make clear here that these samples, like Ford's (1949) surface collections, are not meant as absolute dating for the sites; what I am dating are the sherd samples, not the buildings occurring in the vicinity of the trenches. In some places sampling was broad enough, the sherds abundant enough, and local soil and constructional features simple enough so that our samples might be considered as yielding mean dates and ranges of occupation at a site. These cases will be pointed out in the following discussion.

I might note here an example of the danger of drawing conclusions from small samples and limited excavation at Mesoamerican sites. In 1954 I dug 9 small trenches at Tancah, 4 around the buildings of Group B, 5 in Group A. All samples were extremely small. Excavations on the plaza sides of buildings were not carried down into plaza fill; those on the outside edges were carried to bedrock. Sherds from each group were combined into a single sample. The combined sample from Group B produced 105 sherds, of which 26 were Tulum Buff Paste Censer ware, 3 were Yucatan Slate, and the balance were heavy, coarse, badly eroded Plain ware which at that time I had not placed chronologically. From Group A, I collected 114 sherds, of which half were Tulum Censer ware, 11 were slipped wares (my Tancah Red, and Tancah Variegated), and the balances were the same Plain ware of Group B. The pottery from these trenches included then a few sherds of slipped pottery from pre-Tulum periods, but the overwhelming concentration of Tulum Buff Paste Censer ware led me to conclude that part or even most of the construction at Tancah was associated with the Tulum complex and that Lothrop's dating was basically correct, that is, what we call today the Early post-Classic Period. At that time I conceived of the Tulum ceramic complex as covering the entire post-Classic Period, with two major architectural phases represented by Tancah and Tulum, and had even begun to postulate that the Tulum complex may have been an offshoot of Toltec-Chichen culture rather than Mayapan!

With these defects and dangers in mind we can now proceed to a survey of the 1954 samples and note their chronological positions.

OTHER EAST-COAST SITES

Mulchi. The sample shows a heavy Tulum Period occupation with all the Tulum Period wares represented. Chiquila Censer ware is also present, Mulchi being the farthest point south at which this type of censer ware was collected in quantity. Along with the Tulum Period occupation Tancah Plain is heavily represented, suggesting either a Tancah Group A or B complex period occupation. Curiously enough, slipped wares of the same complex are lacking. Their absence may be due to the fact that our sample is in part from an occupational area, but it may mean that our sample dates from the close of the Group A complex period.

Kilometer 35. The material from this site fits in neatly with our Tulum Period, and we find a heavy representation of Tulum Black Paste Censer, indicating that the site was still going strong at the time of the Conquest. As we shall see shortly, the same is true of many Cozumal Island sites and confirms the Conquest Period accounts as to the importance of Cozumel and the neighboring coast as a religious center. I believe that the samples at this site are definitive as to the mean and range of the date of occupation.

Xelha. The sample, collected from a settlement area surface and a series of trenches along house mounds, shows an interesting parallel to the situation at Tancah. The material suggests a period of heavy occupation running possibly from the closing phase of Group A complex at Tancah through Group B complex, as Tancah Plain, restricted orifice bowls, and Yucatan Slate are present. The Tulum complex representation is lighter and may indicate ceremonial reuse. The architecture, as Lothrop points out, is much closer to Tancah than to Tulum.

Ak 1. This single-shrine site undoubtedly fits entirely with the Tulum Period, especially with the final phase, as indicated by the heavy showing of Tulum Black Paste Censer.

Palmol. This I believe is one of my most poorly sampled sites, and I offer the following sherd dating without much confidence. Our entire sample is of the Tulum Period, but it is based on a single trench dug off the edge of a building which has several constructional periods. My sample presumably represents the final phase of building use and is Tulum Period.

Palmol Playa. At this site a single trench was excavated along the small beam-and-masonry roof temple, and the sherd sample turned out to be of Tulum Period. Although the sample probably dates the structure, it does not necessarily limit the occupation of the site.

NORTH COAST

The close stylistic similarity of Chiquila Censer to Tulum Buff Paste Censer indicates a probable contemporaneity to our Tulum ceramic complex. That complex does not occur in its precise form in this area, but we find close stylistic resemblances in the censer ware, and the presence of Tulum Red, Mayapan Black-on-cream, and V Fine Orange in small quantities, the first with somewhat coarser paste than at Tulum, indicates a closely allied complex.

Yuukluuk. The sample here probable dates the single-shrine site, and it falls entirely in the Tulum Period.

Vista Alegre. This site presents one of the most interesting problems in chronology encountered in the survey. At Vista Alegre we found one deep soil deposit with a heavy sherd concentration which was excavated in three levels. The top level showed abundant evidence of the Tulum complex, and indicates strong occupation of the site for this period. Mixed with the Tulum complex in our sample was a strong secondary occurrence of Vista Alegre Striated ware (17 per cent). In the middle level we find this ware rising to 59 per cent, and finally, in the bottom level, to 74 per cent. It is associated in the lower levels with a secondary concentration of Yucatan Slate ware (6 to 11 per cent). Along with these major wares a few sherds of the later phase of Regional Polychrome (Tepeu) were present.

At Tancah we noted that a few rims of Vista Alegre Striated were associated with a predominately Yucatan Slate-Regional Polychrome-Tancah Plain assemblage. At San Miguel, to be analyzed a little later, we found Vista Alegre Striated again in association with Yucatan Slate but here they occurred almost in equal strength. In other words, if we combine our samples from Tancah and San Miguel with those from this Vista Alegre trench we have a consistent record of the typical Ford (1949) double-ended bomb type of ware distribution. Vista Alegre Striated would seem to begin somewhere during the time of Group B complex and gradually to increase in percentage, reaching its full maximum when Slate ware was declining, and finally to fade off during the Tulum Period.

If this analysis is correct the ware is of great importance, since it may solve, in this local area at least, the problem of the Tula-Toltec or Toltec-Chichen Itza Period, which in central Yucatan is characterized by a highly specialized ceramic and architectural complex limited almost entirely to Chichen Itza. Our analysis suggests that a local regional Maya culture was continuing in the eastern part of the Peninsula during this period and included Vista Alegre Striated with a secondary survival of Yucatan Slate. I offer this reconstruction tentatively; conceivably Vista Alegre Striated may be nothing more than a northern variant of Tancah Striated, and our samples may date with Group B complex at Tancah. Both interpretations are acceptable, although I favor the former.

Cancun Island. The samples from Cancun are almost entirely from the Tulum complex, with Chiquila Censer ware dominating. A few sherds of Yucatan Slate suggest some Group B complex occupation, but if there was, it evidently was very minor. The architecture confirms the Tulum complex dating.

El Meco. The same generalization made for Cancun applies here, and the combination of Yucatan Slate with Vista Alegre Striated may mean an earlier period at El Meco correlating with our postulated Vista Alegre-Yucatan Slate-Early post-Classic Period.

The single-shrine sites called Cocal 1 and 2 yielded only Tulum Period wares, and the buildings undoubtedly date from that period.

Chiquila. The building stratigraphy encountered at Chiquila reveals two separate, unrelated ceramic complexes. The latest, which is post-constructional, is of the Tulum Period in its special north-coast variant. From within the platform fill we find another ceramic assemblage which includes Tancah Plain, Tancah Red (very minor), Chiquila Variegated (a northern variant of Tancah Variegated), and Regional Polychrome. The material closely correlates with that from the final phases of Group A complex at Tancah. The few sherds of Vista Alegre Striated from the third trench imply also some occupation during a later period. It is probable that Chiquila had a longer occupation than the samples indicate, for the site is extensive with a number of separate unsurveyed big pyramids.

COZUMEL ISLAND

San Miguel. In the ceramic assemblage both Slate wares and Vista Alegre Striated are abundant, and also the Tulum complex and Regional Polychrome of the Tzakol type are fairly well represented. The site evidently had a long occupation, running through the Group B complex period and the succeeding Vista Alegre and Tulum periods.

Aguada Grande. This is one of the most puzzling and interesting sites excavated. Practically the entire sample is Aguada Grande Censer ware, which I believe is post-Conquest in date. There is, however, evidence of occupation for the Tulum Period and late Group A, Group B, and Vista

Alegre complex periods as well, so that the site evidently had a long but probably minor use in terms of our ceramic chronology.

San Gervasio. Our samples were from a single palace-type structure where association of the pottery with the building was clear. The pottery represents mostly Tulum Period occupation, including its latest phase.

El Cedral. Samples from this site were very poor. They come from the Group B complex and Tulum periods, including the final phase of the Tulum Period.

Celerain 1. The entire sample from this single-shrine site dates from the final phase of the Tulum Period.

Punta Islote. This is another small shrine site. All the trenches are from the vicinity of a single building, which shows clear evidence of two architectural phases. The ceramic sample also shows two distinct complexes (mixed in the trench, which was shallow). The late phase of the Tulum Period includes the bulk of the sample, but a few sherds indicate a Group B complex period occupation; possibly the inner shrine dates from this earlier time.

Las Grecas. This is one of the most poorly sampled sites excavated. For what the information is worth, the small sample is almost entirely from the final phase of the Tulum Period.

Celerain 2. The sample from this single-shrine site fits entirely into our Tulum Period.

INTERIOR SITES

Kantunil Kin. The major excavation carried on at this site was concerned with building stratigraphy. Sherd samples were collected from a series of superimposed structures, but the total sample does not vary much from level to level and the changes and additions to the original structure seem to have been made within a limited period. Samples show a strong occurrence of Regional Polychrome and Tancah Plain and a lesser amount of Chiquila Variegated. The entire construction seems to equate with the closing phase of our Group A complex.

A plaza trench, on the other hand, yielded mostly Tancah Variegated, and these remains may belong to the immediately preceding phase. Kantunil Kin is a large site and almost surely had a long period of occupation. Our samples show that it was occupied at least during the later part of the Group A complex period.

El Diez. The samples from El Diez run the entire ceramic range from the later part of Group A complex on to the Tulum Period. Sherd frequencies are fairly equal, period by period, and the site was evidently occupied either continuously or intermittently for a long time.

Kilometer 14. The neighboring site of Kilometer 14 presents a somewhat similar picture but with the Tulum and Vista Alegre periods, as well as the earlier phase at El Diez, scantily represented.

Leona Vicario. Our sample from Leona Vicario is decidedly inadequate, but the 68 sherds collected there may represent one of the oldest archaeological complexes in Quintana Roo, as the ceramic assemblage is similar to that from the base levels at Tancah.

Santa Maria. This site also is poorly sampled. The small sample indicates possibly two phases of occupation: one toward the end of Group A complex, the other during the Vista Alegre period.

Solfarino. Our sample from Solfarino is almost entirely Tulum Period in date with a few sherds of the Vista Alegre complex.

Monte Bravo. The samples from this site seem to show a long period of occupation, running from the end of Group B complex times to the Vista Alegre period, with a few sherds of the Tulum Period.

THE CERAMIC COLUMN FOR NORTHERN QUINTANA ROO

By combining the results from a number of sites I have tentatively set up a ceramic chronological column (chart 3) for the northern half of the Territory as follows:

The Tancah complex includes all the material from our Group A trenches at Tancah and is the earliest ceramic assemblage found in the area. It is best represented at Tancah itself. A series of three phases can be set up and called Phases A, B, and C.

The San Miguel complex includes the material from our Group B complex at Tancah and is named after the first site where Yucatan Slate occurred in abundance. No phases have been defined in it to date.

The Vista Alegre complex represents the most problematic of our periods; I suggest it tentatively as a true chronological phase bridging the gap between San Miguel and Tulum. It is that period in which Vista Alegre Striated reaches its maximum importance as a ware and occurs in conjunction with Yucatan Slate. Conceivably the period might be divided into an A and a B phase, Yucatan Slate decreasing in frequency from A to B, but the suggestion is advanced as a hypothesis only.

The Tulum complex marks one of the most clearly defined periods and enjoys a huge spatial range even running as far south as southern Quintana Roo and northern British Honduras. It may be divided into two phases: A, the main period, embracing most of the total time range; and B, a brief period ending shortly after the Conquest and characterized by Tulum Black Paste Censer.

The Aguada Grande complex includes the material from the site of Aguada Grande. It may be Colonial in date.

Chart 3 attempts to show the estimated time span of the wares defined in this study and the dating of our site samples.

A number of observations are pertinent. First of all, we have clear evidence for a great expansion of activity during the Tulum Period along the immediate coast. Only Tancah, Xelha, San Miguel, El Cedral, and Vista Alegre show evidence of heavy building and occupation before the Tulum Period. The east coast evidently played a key role in northern Yucatecan culture during this period. Inland sites, on the other hand, tend to be earlier in their periods of maximal prosperity, as nearly as our limited sample can indicate. Interestingly enough, all the sites that show important occupation in the final phase of the Tulum Period are on Cozumel Island or just opposite it on the neighboring mainland, thus checking neatly with the documentary evidence.

During the Tulum Period an over-all cultural unity is apparent, especially in the field of

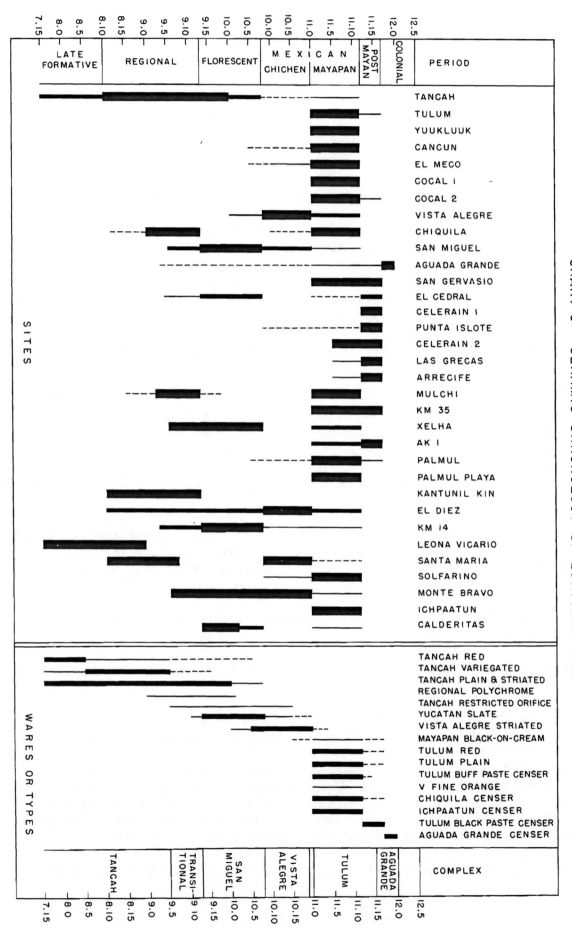

religion and its symbolic manifestations (censer wares, architecture), but there are spatial provinces within this over-all unity. The northern half of the Territory may be divided into two areas: that north of Mulchi and Puerto Morelos, and that south of them. As we shall see shortly in our discussion of the Chetumal area, southern Quintana Roo also forms an identifiable subregion.

To a certain extent these regional subdivisions may be extended backward, but here we are on shaky ground because of the small number of sites with pre-Tulum material. We do find, however, that Tancah Variegated characterizes the southern area, Chiquila Variegated the northern, and that Vista Alegre Striated, regardless of its dating, is rare in the south and much more common in the north.

ARCHITECTURE

No attempt will be made in this report to work out the history of east-coast architecture, but a few observations may offer guidance for future work in this direction. The distinctive style defined exhaustively by Lothrop is much older than the Tulum Period; it goes back to the beginnings, or nearly to the beginnings, of our ceramic charts. Tancah and Xelha represent the older phases of this tradition, Tulum the newer. This much I think is clear in spite of the lack of stratigraphic data in our two site studies. The isolated shrine seems in general to be late, but I doubt that it was entirely absent in the early phases. The columned palace seems exclusively a Tulum Period form.

8. QUINTANA ROO AND THE LOWLAND MAYA AREA

In the preceding section I discussed the chronology of the east coast of Yucatan, defining five major periods and a number of phases. In this section I will attempt to relate this chronology to sequences from elsewhere in the lowland Maya area. In certain respects this is a fairly simple problem; in others it is rather difficult. The basic outlines of the cross ties seem clear; it is in more detailed ware resemblances and dating that the problem becomes exceedingly complex.

I cannot here go into the morass of ceramic interrelationships that characterize the huge area called the lowland Maya, but I will point out a number of clear-cut resemblances between wares and periods outside the east-coast area from the chronological point of view rather than from that of ware origin or of functional and genetic linkages among wares. The fact that northeastern Yucatan is a geographical and hence historical cul-de-sac simplifies our study. Strong cultural influences must of necessity have come either from the States of Yucatan and Campeche to the west or from the Department of Peten to the south. Unfortunately, however, although the ceramics of northern Yucatan are well known and have been studied by competent field men, no full report of the material is available for comparison and citation. Among the Carnegie Institution collections in Merida is a considerable volume of sherd material from all over the state of Yucatan, and a lesser amount from Campeche, but very little of it has been adequately studied and published. I have used this material extensively for cross dating, but lack of publication means that the reader will have to take on faith some of my statements of relationships. Many of my references for Yucatecan wares are derived from surveys by the late George Brainerd, as yet unpublished, for this important archaeological region. (The Archaeological Ceramics of Yucatan, by G. W. Brainerd [Univ. Calif., Anthropol. Records, vol. 19, Berkeley and Los Angeles, 1958], had not appeared when the present report was submitted.—Editor) Also, the Carnegie Institution has been carrying out extensive testing in recent years in the same area, and the material is being studied and analyzed by R. E. Smith. Smith in personal discussion and communication has presented chronological views at variance with Brainerd's, thus creating another problem in handling and presenting my material. These disagreements will be pointed out in the text in the course of the discussion and will be noted in the ware descriptions in the Appendix.

South of our area we are more fortunate, as well worked out sequences have been published for Benque Viejo, San Jose, Holmul, Uaxactun, and Copan. Unfortunately, however, Smith's (1955) final Uaxactun report had not been published when the laboratory study of the Quintana Roo materials was made, so that exact ware comparisons with his material are impossible.

Our Quintana Roo sequence is based on the seriation of a number of wares which for the most part have clearly defined historical limits. In this discussion, therefore, I will first emphasize ware relationships with outside material and then correlate the time position of our periods with other established sequences.

TULUM PERIOD WARES

Tulum Period Censer Ware (fig. 7,c,d; fig. 8). This general ware included in our ceramic breakdown such types as Tulum Buff Paste Censer, Tulum Black Paste Censer, Chiquila Censer, and Ichpaatun Censer, all closely interrelated and varying only in surface and paste. Ladle censers occur in all.

The typical censer is the full-figure pedestal-base form. As far as I know, in northern

Yucatan such censers are limited to the post-Classic period. They occur at both Chichen Itza and Mayapan. All the following characteristics are present in the Chichen Itza censer, the Mayapan censer, and the Tulum Period censers: pedestal bases; pierced bases and walls; tall vase-like vessel bodies with direct rims; buttons applied as adornos on vessels without figurines; standing male figurine (except at Chiquila, where all are female) portrayed often with stiff, straight lower limbs and arms bent forward from the elbow, the hands holding copal balls or other objects; fanged faces; elaborately decorated figures and with standard forms of plumes, buttons, fans, and rectangular back ornaments or wings which are almost duplicated in exact detail from ware to ware and applied on the figure; painting of the figurine and vessel in plaster-like paints; the application of a ribbon of clay around the vessel just above the pedestal base with fingernail impressions on the ribbon.

The only important respect in which the east-coast wares diverge in form from censer from Chichen Itza is the frequent occurrence of bolstered rims both on the vessel and on the pedestal base; in paste and surface, as far as I could tell, Tulum Buff Paste Censer and Mayapan Censer are indistinguishable. Chichen Itza censer ware seems to be limited to the tall, vertical-walled vessel (vase type in the preceding comparison), whereas at Mayapan we find vessels with more flaring sides and jars very close in shape to the east-coast variants. Some censers from Mayapan have the typical east-coast rim bolster.

In general I believe that the closest ties of Quintana Roo are with Mayapan rather than Chichen Itza in the full-figure, pedestal-base form of censer. In Tulum Buff Paste Censer we find a cuplike censer with tripod legs and also a small animal effigy incense burner with cuplike upper part and pedestal base (fig.8,a,10, b,30). Both these forms occur commonly at Mayapan though not as censers. I think that the correlation in period is clear. The east-coast censer wares probably are of the Mayapan Period. The simple open-ended tubular censer handle that we noted for the east-coast group is found also at Mayapan.

We have mentioned previously the great spatial distribution of the Tulum Complex. It occurs along the entire coast of Quintana Roo from Chiquila in the north to Chetumal in the south. As a complex it does not seem to occur outside of the coastal strip of the territory. Certain elements of the complex, however, do occur in northern British Honduras at Santa Rita (Gann, 1900). A close similarity in the style of the murals from Santa Rita to those from Tulum has been noted by several authors, indicating a contemporaneity of the two sites.

In the course of his excavations Gann collected some pottery, and his report illustrates a number of vessels that almost duplicate the style and forms of our Tulum censer ware. Plate XXXII in his report shows figurines that are so close in style to our specimens from Tulum as to be indistinguishable from them, and illustrations 5 and 6 on plate XXXIII are very close to one of our Tulum effigy jars (fig. 15,i).

Tulum Red Ware, Bowl Forms. Tripod basal break bowls with red slip are common in northern Yucatan, and the basic form has a long time range. It occurs at the Florescent Period Puuc sites, where Brainerd calls the ware Puuc Red; at Chichen Itza, where he has defined the ware as Chichen Red; and it is also present at Mayapan. Tulum Red ware basal break bowls are distinctive from basal break bowls in any of the above wares, and Tulum Red must be defined as a separate ware. It has close resemblances to Mayapan Red, but Tulum Red ware in general is of finer paste and has a faster slip than Mayapan Red, although in the last trait it is much closer to Mayapan than to either Puuc or Chichen Red. The tendency toward flaking is present in both Mayapan and Tulum Red, and many sherds from Tulum have partly or completely lost their slip. Ichpaatun samples of Tulum Red ware, on the other hand, are superior in this respect to sherds from either Mayapan or Tulum. Slip color is very close, and it is almost impossible to separate

Tulum and Mayapan body sherds, except perhaps by paste, and frequently the wares overlap. Basal break bowls with basal flanges are rare at Mayapan. Some basal break bowls at Mayapan have effigy supports. Effigy supports are not definitely linked with this form on the east coast, but they occur in Tulum Red ware. Mayapan Red has a variety of forms in supports. One vessel, which I thought might be a trade piece from the east coast but which Shook stated was definitely Mayapan Red, has the typical Tulum pierced tubular support. Solid cylindrical supports of the same shape as those at Tulum are rather common at Mayapan, and subglobular hollow pierced supports with rattles, also common at Mayapan, occur at Tulum in small numbers. In summary, the supports overlap, but the emphasis on particular forms is different in the two wares (fig. 4,a,b,c).

Hemispherical bowls, including chile graters, with supports, occur at Mayapan. At Tulum some bowls of this type lack supports (fig. 4,d). The Mayapan examples are generally heavier, thicker-walled vessels.

Jar Forms. In Tulum Red ware we define three jar types, all of which are closely approximated in Mayapan Red. Our wide-mouthed, direct rim, low-necked form and also the coarse paste, high-necked, narrow-mouthed form with bolstered rims can be duplicated at Mayapan. The type we are calling Flaring Rim High-Necked jar is very close to what R. E. Smith calls Parenthesis Rim jar (fig. 5).

Exotic Forms. One vessel from Mayapan almost duplicates our effigy jar with the pedestal base from Tulum. Both are jar forms with pedestal bases and have an appliquéd series of steps added to the body of the vessel just above the pedestal base (fig. 15,d). The effigy face, however, is lacking from the Mayapan vessel. Lamp-chimney forms are also common to both areas (fig. 5,f, 1,2).

Of interest is a vessel of Mayapan Red ware found at Mayapan with a modeled diving god figure applied—a clear link between Tulum and the former site. The modeling of the figurines from ware to ware reveals very close stylistic links.

One of the major distinctions between Tulum and Mayapan Red, especially with respect to the Ichpaatun sample, is the amount of incised decoration; it is rare at Mayapan, fairly common at Tulum, and common at Ichpaatun.

In general our comparison indicates that Tulum Red is a distinct ware in its own right but shows close ties with Mayapan Red in the state of Yucatan. (According to a personal communication from H. E. D. Pollock, sherds of Tulum Red have been found at Mayapan. We also understand that A. O. Shepard has found Tulum Red to be different in temper [dolomite] from Mayapan Red.)

Tulum Plain (fig. 6,b,c,d,e). At Mayapan occurs a ware called Mayapan Unslipped which is almost identical with Tulum Plain. As far as I can tell, the wares are indistinguishable in form and surface treatment and similar in paste. The only noticeable difference is that some of the Mayapan examples are very lightly raked, whereas none of the Tulum specimens are.

Mayapan Black-on-Cream. Ware resemblances are so close here that I have simply labeled my sample from Tulum and other east-coast sites Mayapan Black-on-cream.

Fine Orange. Berlin (1956) in a recently published study of Fine Orange ware in Tabasco has defined two new types of Fine Orange other than Brainerd's (1941) original X and Z. He calls them U and V. Both are chronologically late post-Classic, with U falling about the time of the Spanish Conquest and being later than V. Excluding small amounts of X and Z, all the classifiable Fine Orange from Mayapan is of V type. The small, often fragmentary, samples of Fine Orange collected from the east-coast sites also fall entirely within Berlin's V Fine Orange type, as nearly as can be told, again checking with our dating of the Tulum Period as contemporary with Mayapan. See ware description for further details.

VISTA ALEGRE COMPLEX

Of great interest, and, I think, significant, in spite of the relatively small number of tested sites, is the fact that no clear-cut ceramic complex of the Early post-Classic or Toltec-Chichen Period was found in Quintana Roo. In reality, as I have pointed out, remains of that period are almost entirely limited to the site of Chichen Itza, a kind of isolated highland Mexican stronghold in an area where the old Maya Classic culture possibly remained constant in surrounding centers. For Quintana Roo I suspect but cannot prove that the Vista Alegre complex spans this period with Vista Alegre Striated and a late persistence of Yucatan Slate. As I have not been able to find wares related to Vista Alegre Striated anywhere in Yucatan, its chronological position cannot be resolved by typological resemblances to outside areas. Striated plain wares in general are common in Yucatan throughout the Classic Period, but the specific ware Vista Alegre Striated seems to be limited to Quintana Roo.

SAN MIGUEL COMPLEX

The complex I have called San Miguel, on the other hand, has definite relationships outside Quintana Roo. This assemblage includes as its dominant wares Yucatan Medium Slate and Thin Slate. Both these types are widespread throughout northern Yucatan.

The types have been studied and broken down in a number of subtypes by Brainerd and Smith, working independently. The author's material was compared in Merida in 1955 with samples from Brainerd's and Smith's surveys without the benefit of knowing what either of their respective classifications were except for some typewritten copies of Brainerd's original laboratory notes. Since then Brainerd's report has been published and there are disagreements with his original notes available to the author and also with work done later by Smith. Since four years have now gone by and the samples are no longer available to the present author my comparisons will have to be very general.

One fact that seems definite is that the Quintana Roo samples fall into two clearly defined types, Medium Slate and Thin Slate, which differ in wall thickness, fineness of paste, and shapes, and both these types are very close to samples from Puuc sites and perhaps fit Brainerd's Florescent Period Medium Slateware and Thin Slate types best. The sample of rim of Medium Slate from Quintana Roo sites shows a relatively small number of forms. A common form is the basin with heavy bolstered rim. Basal break bowls are the most common form, and they have low rectangular slab solid supports and fingernail-impressed decoration just above the exterior basal angle. In Brainerd's laboratory notes he states that this form tends to have an eastern distribution in Yucatan. A final form is the bolstered rim high-necked jar decorated by vertically painted parallel stripes, usually brown to black. In this report we have separated this and called it Black on Slate. This feature also occurs in samples from Yucatan.

Even more serious in terms of our interpretation of Quintana Roo chronology is the sharp disagreement between Brainerd and Smith on the dating of this group of "slate wares."

Brainerd (1956, pp. 163) makes the following statement:

"The Puuc area is a particularly favorable region for the study of settlement patterns. Ceremonial architecture is extremely common and well preserved there; preservation is good because the region has been lightly inhabited for the last thousand years. The four largest of the Puuc sites—Uxmal, Kabah, Sayil, and Labna—have been sampled archaeologically. They extend in almost a straight northwest-southeast line, about 20 miles from end to end; Uxmal, the largest, is also the furthest separated of the group. The four sites are contemporary; they were occupied from about A.D. 700 to 1000. This is a far shorter time span than that found for any other of the 20 major sites sampled in Yucatan, all of which show occupations of over 1000 years in length."

The type ware for these sites and period is Yucatan Slate (Puuc variety), and Brainerd in general would date it as Late Classic or Yucatan Florescent. Smith, on the other hand, in personal discussion and communication states that most of these sites and Yucatan Medium Slate ware may go back to Early Classic and in any case to Brainerd's Regional Period.

We will return to this chronological argument shortly.

The sudden appearance of Yucatan Slate wares, and the abandonment of Group A and possible later construction of Group B at Tancah, argue for an actual movement of peoples from Yucatan into the Tancah region and a subsequent introduction of new religious concepts, although the point cannot be stressed strongly until building stratigraphy is attempted at Tancah.

REGIONAL POLYCHROME

Brainerd's survey of the State of Yucatan produced a ware that he calls Regional Polychrome. R. E. Smith in an examination of the material considers it almost identical with the polychrome painted Peten Gloss ware of the Tzakol period. Inasmuch as my material from Quintana Roo cannot be distinguished from the Yucatecan lots, I am using Brainerd's ware designation of Regional Polychrome. The only problem, therefore, is the exact chronological position of my sherd samples with respect to Smith's Peten sequence.

Brainerd dates his Yucatecan sample as Middle Regional, contemporary with Tzakol and just preceding the earliest Yucatan Medium Slate ware.

By far the predominant form in Quintana Roo is the basal flange bowl, which in shape, color combination, and design is almost identical with Smith's Tzakol period Peten Gloss ware (Smith, 1955, fig. 25). In some of our samples, such as the very small ones from Kantunil Kin, this was the only form. In his discussion of chronology at Uaxactun, Smith indicates that an important difference between Tzakol 1 and 2-3 lies in the percentage of this form; it seems to increase from the earlier to the later period. Consequently, although our samples are statistically small, I believe it significant that this is always the most popular form except for specimens from some trenches at Tancah which I shall discuss shortly.

A monochrome (orange slip) vessel of Peten Gloss ware that is illustrated and labeled by Smith as a Z-angle bowl (ibid., fig. 18,a,1) is identical in form with our burial vessel from Tancah (fig. 15,1). This is a rare shape in our sample and is not diagnostic of any particular phase of the over-all Tzakol Period.

Round-sided bowls in this ware are very close to similar vessels from Uaxactun that Smith dates as Tzakol 2-3, Tepeu 1 (ibid., fig. 34).

At Tancah, Regional Polychrome samples show a wider range of shape and seem to include not only Tzakol but Tepeu forms as well. Many of our trenches from the area west of Group B produced samples in which both Regional Polychrome and Yucatan Slate were abundant., It must be remembered, of course, that the samples are from shallow, unstratified, mixed deposits often unassociated with buildings; but even so I suspect that Yucatan Slate and Regional Polychrome are contemporary in part, at least during the final phase of the latter ware's popularity in the area. There is an abundance of Tepeu forms in these trenches from Tancah; many of our samples of Tzakol Period Regional Polychrome from other sites in Quintana Roo reveal no slate ware at all; and the Tzakol Period sherds are mixed with Chiquila Variegated at Kantunil Kin and Chiquila. Tepeu forms include the lateral-ridged bowls or dishes which at Uaxactun are dated by Smith (1955, fig. 36) as Tepeu 1, polychrome flaring-sided bowls (often with flat bases) also dated as Tepeu 1 (ibid., fig. 35,b), and a few sherds of red and black on cream flat-bottomed bowls which are very common at Calderitas and are Tepeu 2 in date.

At San Jose, Thompson's (1939) lateral-ridged bowls dating from period 3 (which immediately succeeds San Jose 2 with its typical Tzakol basal flange bowls) are very similar to our lateral-ridged sherds from Tancah.

Curiously absent from Quintana Roo are a number of typical Tepeu traits such as barrel-shaped vases, figure painting, and tripod supports of any kind.

My over-all impression is that the Regional Polychrome of northern Quintana Roo dates from Tzakol 2 to Tepeu 2, with most of the material falling in Tzakol 3, Tepeu 1. It is an important ware chronologically, since it occurs in association with both Tancah and San Miguel complex assemblages and tends to link them.

TANCAH COMPLEX

The earliest ceramic assemblage defined for Quintana Roo is what we are calling the Tancah complex, which has been stratigraphically placed at the site of Tancah itself. It includes two slipped types, Tancah Red and Tancah Variegated, along with two plain wares, Tancah Plain and Tancah Striated. Tancah Red and Tancah Variegated seem very similar in slip, form, and decoration to Brainerd's Late Formative slipped ware. In his short 1951 article (pp. 74-75) he states:

"The collections of the Late Formative substage from the various sites show variation, some of it probably regional, some certainly chronological. I shall give a general description. The predominant ware is slipped monochrome red, orange, white, gray, or black. Often the exterior and interior colors are markedly and certainly intentionally different. Colors show some correlation with vessel forms. The slip at most sites is closely adherent. The pottery of the Late Formative period shows on the average considerably thicker walls than that of the preceding periods. The predominant form is a heavy, large, flat-bottomed bowl with flaring sides, often with everted flat lip. Other forms include small-shouldered jars, round-sided vessels of various sorts, cuspidor-shaped vessels, and globular jars with notch neck. A few large hollow legs occur sporadically. Most sites show a few spouts. There is one flat fabric stamp and one appliquéd hand-modeled face from a vessel side. Occasional flanges are found placed sub-labially and on vessel sides. Decoration includes very rare blobs of red paint, and much pale trickle paint occurs at some sites. This paint sometimes gives a resist effect, and sometimes is darker than the ground color. A fragment of Usulutan ware occurs. Vessels are decorated by incising and grooving in a considerable variety of patterns: fluting both horizontal and vertical, fingernail impression, impression by a reed or similar hollow circular tool. Decoration in several cases varies significantly between sites. Minor wares include at some sites red slipped over striated jars, at some a thin and highly polished orange ware, but no burnished orange-brown ware like that of the Middle Formative period. Unslipped striated jars form a minor constituent of the samples. Altogether the variety of forms and decoration of this period is somewhat greater than in those that follow.''

Moving further afield, my Tancah slipped wares and Brainerd's Yucatan Late Formative slipped ware are so close to Smith's Chicanel Waxy Monochrome that separate identification is almost impossible. Smith examined my collections in the Merida office. In a personal communication he states:

''I have been over your Tancah Red and Tancah Bichrome [Variegated]. There is absolutely no doubt in my mind that both are pre-Classic wares essentially Chicanel in every respect. In my judgment you have included in your Tancah Bichrome [Variegated] many Tancah Red sherds that show the result of fire-clouding or differences of temperature in baking which vary the slip color. These features are all part of Chicanel Waxy Red ware. Now since I have gone over your material in more detail I find that you do have a rather small but definite collection of a two color ware. This I have called Red-on-buff and described on page 33 of my book. Note the color range of the buff. I found one sherd (Q-206) of this type with vertical (slightly curved at ends) red stripes or lines and dots (Smith, 1955, fig. 70,c,5). Your Red-on-buff and Tancah Red sherds can be duplicated in almost every case in my Chicanel illustrations (figs. 16 and 70).

''In my opinion you have in your Tancah Red and Tancah Bichrome [Variegated] exactly what I had in the Chicanel Phase at Uaxactun with Chicanel Waxy Red and Chicanel Waxy Red-on-buff.''

All the shape and slip-color variations noted for my Tancah wares occur in Smith's Chicanel illustrations (see R. E. Smith, 1955, fig. 16).

Tancah Striated and Plain show closest outside resemblances in lip form to Smith's Chicanel Unslipped storage jars, which also have raked or striated surfaces (ibid., fig. 16,a,b).

From purely typological arguments, therefore, our Tancah complex looks as though it fits entirely into the Late Formative Period, in spite of strong arguments in favor of extending the complex well into the Early Classic or Brainerd's Regional Period. The reasons for my position are numerous.

First, the Regional Period all over the State of Yucatan includes a number of local red slipped wares such as Regional Medium Paste Red, Regional Coarse Paste Red, and Flaky Red, all defined by Brainerd (unpublished) and all common at Coba in the Territory and only 30 miles from the east coast. Brainerd states that there is considerable similarity in paste and slip between these wares and Late Formative Monochrome, and that the main criterion for sorting is shape. Farther south in Quintana Roo we noted a local red slipped ware we are calling Calderitas Red. Therefore it would seem curious, in view of this widespread distribution of local red slipped wares over the Peninsula all around our northeast coastal area during the Regional Period, to find no local variety on the coast itself. In sampling about 40 sites some material from the Early Regional Period should have turned up; yet all we have are Tancah Red and Tancah Variegated. It is possible, of course, that our 40 sites constituted too small a sampling to include sites of this period. (Most of the Regional Period red slipped wares are characterized by a very flaky slip. In checking over my samples R. E. Smith noted that some of the badly eroded sherds classed as Tancah Plain may actually be a badly weathered type of local red ware from this period.)

Second, and I believe that this argument is even stronger, all the big samples from Tancah in which Tancah Red and Tancah Variegated dominate were taken from in and around Group A. Very few other wares are represented in these samples, Regional Polychrome being exceedingly rare.

The only exception is, of course, the post-constructional remains from the Tulum period population, which is strictly a top-soil assemblage. Many of our typologically Formative samples are associated with plaza floor constructions. There are two possible explanations for this last situation: either the floor levels are actually Late Formative in date, or the fill between and on the floor is occupational debris gathered from outlying earlier sites which was used as fill material by the later population during the Regional period. Neither of these arguments is really very convincing. For one thing, although there is masonry architecture associated with the Late Formative period in other parts of the Lowland Maya area, it is simple in type with only platforms and pyramids and no corbeled roofing; the buildings of Group A, however, are of fully developed east-coast style with all the forms of Classic Maya architecture. For another, even if the bulk of the pottery is from fill scooped up from older sites, we should expect to find Regional Period refuse on the plaza floors dating from the use of the surrounding buildings; yet we do not, and what Regional Polychrome pottery is found is rare and occurs only between the first two floors in our plaza trenches.

A third reason for not considering the Tancah complex to belong exclusively to the Late Formative Period is as follows. Although Smith in his report on Uaxactun does not utilize seriation in breaking down his Chicanel Period, his chart on decorated sherds seems to indicate a predominance of Red over Variegated and other slip colors as in our bottom levels of the Tancah complex trenches. Our levels in which the trend is reversed might well represent a persistence of Chicanel-like forms and wares into the Early Regional Period in our area.

Finally, some of the lip forms in Chiquila Variegated and Tancah Red seem to be more closely allied to Coba Red than to the Formative slipped wares. I refer specifically to the thickened rims which are especially common in Chiquila Variegated. In this connection it is interesting that the latter ware is often found in low frequencies associated with Regional Polychrome (as at Chiquila and Kantunil Kin). It may be that most of my Tancah Variegated is Late Formative and that the Chiquila Variegated is later and therefore has chronological rather than spatial significance as compared with Tancah Variegated.

Although I freely admit that these conclusions are based on small, at times inadequate, samples, I tentatively suggest the chronological ordering of my Quintana Roo material as indicated in chart 3.

CHETUMAL AREA POTTERY

The correlation of our northern Quintana Roo periods with other sequences from the Maya area, then, seems fairly well resolved, and it remains only to establish the relationships between the Chetumal material and other regions. Logically, our Chetumal wares should show close resemblances to the well worked out sequences from San Jose (Thompson, 1939) and Benque Viejo (Thompson, 1940) in British Honduras, and to a certain extent they do. Of great interest, however, is the complete lack of Tulum Period (represented by our material from Ichpaatun) pottery from either of those sites, indicating possibly that British Honduras along with the Peten suffered a drastic population decline after the Classic Period. Ichpaatun might be considered the most southern outpost of post-Classic culture in the Peninsula. Modifying this picture somewhat is the previously noted case of Santa Rita, but that site is located in northern British Honduras only a mile from the coast.

Our material from Calderitas, on the other hand, shows definite relationships to Thompson's San Jose IV-V Periods.

At San Jose we find a long tradition of Slipped Red ware manufacture, but our Calderitas Red is distinct in form except for some of the dishes or comal shapes; these, however, have a long time span at San Jose and are not diagnostically significant. Calderitas Red evidently is related to San Jose Red wares only in a generic sense and apparently represents another local regional ceramic complex within the lowland Maya area. Calderitas Fine Paste Striated seems to be absent from other Maya sequences and to be a peculiarly local development.

Our closest ties with San Jose are in the ware I have called Calderitas Polychrome. Fortunately this ware has a limited time range at San Jose, dating entirely from Period IV and at Benque Viejo from Phase IIIb. Some of Thompson's photographs of this ware from Benque Viejo (there called Polychrome on Whitish Background) are very similar to our Calderitas Polychrome. Our Calderitas Black ware also shows close similarity in slip, shape, and use of fluted decoration to his San Jose Black ware, which again is most common in Period IV. Add to these resemblances the extremely close similarity in San Jose IV and V Unslipped Jar Rims to our Calderitas Striated, and the chronological position of our samples is clear. Of interest is the fact that Yucatan Slate occurs as a minor ware in our upper level at Calderitas and appears at San Jose in Period V.

Theoretically, then, the Calderitas sample may be divided into two phases, one definitely correlating with San Jose IV, the other with V. Actually the lack of carved ware and supports, both diagnostic traits of Period V at San Jose, might indicate entirely a Period IV correlation for both our phases at Calderitas. Quite possibly slate wares might have arrived earlier at Calderitas than at San Jose.

This correlation is checked neatly by comparison with Smith's sequence at Uaxactun. Here he has a variety of Peten Gloss ware that he has called red-and-black-on-cream which is identical in form and color combination to our Calderitas Polychrome. At Uaxactun its chronological position is Tepeu 2 (Smith, fig. 39,16,19,22,23).

9. APPENDIX A   POTTERY WARES

TULUM COMPLEX WARES

Tulum Red Ware (figs. 4; 5; 6,a; 15,a-c,e; 18,e,f)

Tulum Red, one of the most distinctive of all Quintana Roo wares, is also one of our best horizon markers, as it seems to have been made during a very restricted period (not over two centuries) and was in widespread use over most of the Territory. Our analysis is based on large collections, which include numerous restorable vessels, from both Tulum and Ichpaatun.

Form

My discussion of this ware will be organized by form, since to a great extent variations in paste, surface treatment, and decoration depend on the form of the vessel involved. In general the bulk of the sherds are from a few limited forms, with little variation. They are as follows:

Basal Break Bowls (figs. 4,a,b; 15,a-c). The basal break is one of the commonest shapes of Tulum Red. The angle of the break is consistently wide, averaging about 150 degrees, and the walls flare outward rather sharply. Bottoms are convex, and the lips of the vessels are simple unbolstered or direct. Typical of this form is a highly distinctive tripod support. The three feet are hollow, cylindical, and flat-bottomed, and they are pierced by one to three small round vents, usually two on the exterior side and one on the interior. Less common types of support are described under Miscellaneous Features. From a number of reconstructable vessels the metric data of the following table were obtained.

Vessel	Rim Diameter (cm)	Bowl Depth (cm)	Total Height (cm)
Tulum			
Q 166 (incised)	19	6.5	8
Q 152	21	8	9.2
Q 155	22	6	Support missing
Q 175	21.8	7.3	8.7
Q 186	24.2	7.6	9
Q 192	22.2	7.5	9
Q 134	26	6.9	9.3
Q 134	25.8	8.8	10.5
Ichpaatun			
Q 308	24	5.8	7.8
Q 300 (incised)	24	5.9	Support missing
Q 328	21.3	7.1	9
Q 312	23.8	5	8.9
Q 300 (incised)	25	6.4	9.4
Q 300	22	6.8	9
Q 300	22	5.9	7.7

Basal Break Bowls with Basal Flanges (fig. 4,c). In general size, proportion, and shape these bowls are very similar to those just discussed, the main distinguishing feature being a sharp protrud-

237

ing flange that extends out from the body of the vessel either at the basal break or slightly above it. The flange runs all the way around the vessel, and it usually has vertical parallel-line incisions at regular intervals scratched on the outer surface of the flange. Only one sherd shows a correlation of this shape with a tripod support, but it seems probable that all vessels carried them. One restorable vessel of this shape (minus supports but with the scar of supports present) recovered at Tulum had a rim diameter of 23 cm and a bowl depth of 6.5 cm (fig. 4,c,15).

Hemispherical Bowls (fig. 4,d). This is a minor shape at both Tulum and Ichpaatun but somewhat more common at Ichpaatun. Two subtypes may be defined. (a) Molcajetes or chile grinders with heavier walls and rasped floors. A restorable vessel (figs. 4,d,13; 15,e) of this type found at Tulum had a rim diameter of 24 cm, a bowl depth of 7.7 cm, and a total height (the vessel has typical Tulum supports) of 8.8 cm. Another almost complete profile sherd from Tulum also has a typical tripod support (fig. 4,d,16). (b) Round-sided bowls, often very small, with thin, delicate walls and incised decoration running in a narrow band just below the rim (fig. 4,d). One of these vessels has a solid conical support.

Direct Rim Jars (fig. 5,d,e). No completely restorable vessels of this form were found, but the sherds are large enough to estimate their shape with some certainty. These jars have relatively thin walls, in comparison with other types of jars, and some have incised decoration. Necks are characteristically very low, slightly to moderately flaring, the rim direct, and the mouth very wide. Bodies are globular, often rather squat, and bases are flat or slightly concave.

Two almost restorable vessels, both with incised decoration, will serve as examples of this shape. Vessel 1 (fig. 5,e,19) has a rim diameter of 16.3 cm, a neck height of 3 cm, and a total vessel height (flat base) of 12 cm. A second vessel (fig. 5,e,3) with the base missing has a calculated rim diameter of 14.2 cm, a neck height of 2.1 cm, and a total vessel height of 10.7 cm. A third vessel is divergent in form with a straight vertical neck and bolstered rim (fig. 5,e,4), but paste and surface treatment correlate with this type rather than with the true bolstered-rim jar of Tulum. This vessel has a rim diameter of 12.2 cm, a neck height of 3.2 cm, and a total height (including small tubular supports) of 9.7 cm.

Vessels of this shape have a considerable range in size: some miniature forms were probably not over 7 cm in height; larger vessels probably measured up to 25 cm. Measurable rim diameters, including those vessels already described, range from 12 to 34 cm; neck heights, from 1.5 to 5 cm.

Flaring-Rim High-Necked Jars (fig. 5,c). (Mayapan Parenthesis Rim jars). This is one of the most distinctive jar shapes in Tulum Red ware. The neck is built in two sections, a lower almost vertical segment and an upper which flares sharply outward (fractures often occur at the junction). The neck was evidently made separately from the body, as shoulder-neck fractions are common. A number of complete necks were collected but no complete or restorable vessel. The necks probably go with larger vessels than the direct rim jars; the jars are higher and less squat in over-all proportions; probably, also, many of the strap handles and concave bases go with this form. They are true jars, very likely used for water storage, with narrower mouth openings and higher necks in proportion to body height than in the direct rim type, which are more nearly necked bowls than jars.

From Tulum and Ichpaatun the reconstructable necks were tabulated as shown.

Vessel	Rim Diameter (cm)	Lower Segment Height (cm)	Total Height (cm)
Tulum			
1	19	5	9.7
2		3.3	6.9
3		6	11
4		4.7	8.2
5		4	8
6		6	10.2
7		6.6	11.5
8	20	6.5	12
Ichpaatun			
1	18.5	5	8.5
2		5	8.2
3		5	8.5
4	17	4.2	6.8
5		3	6
6		3.7	6.7
7		5.5	9.5
8	17	4.5	6.9
9		5.7	8.5
10		5	7.8

Bolstered Rim Jars (fig. 5,a). At both Tulum and Ichpaatun this is a much rarer form than either direct rim or flaring rim jars. At Tulum, bolstered rim jars generally are larger, higher-necked vessels, with much thicker walls and coarser paste than the direct rim type, and with coarser paste than the flaring rim. At Ichpaatun many are similar technically to the flaring rim type and lack the coarse paste quality of the Tulum jars. At both sites they are high-necked vessels. Tulum rims have a round, short bolster; those from Ichpaatun, a more elongated, flatter one. The Tulum sample of this shape shows a close similarity to slipped examples of Chiquila Censer from sites farther north, and very often samples from these north-coast sites (Cancun, El Meco, Chiquila, Vista Alegre) include no other form of red slipped jars. It would perhaps be more feasible to group all slipped Chiquila Censer ware with the Tulum coarse paste red into a single ware type; under this classification the Ichpaatun bolstered rim jars would be a unique form under Tulum Red, restricted, as far as our samples show, to that site. (See Chiquila Censer Ware for further description.)

Exotic Forms. At both Tulum and Ichpaatun were found a number of rare vessel forms in Tulum Red ware which fall into three major types: vasiform, effigy, and multiple-mouth jars. Vasiform types generally are small vessels, often with small vertical loop handles and very thin walls, with incised decoration, and of "lamp-chimney" form with high, straight vertical necks and globular bodies (fig. 5,f,1-16). Basal forms are not known.

Two effigy vessels, almost complete, which were evidently placed one on either side of the stairway of Structure 25 in the angle formed by the stairs and the platform wall, were recovered from Tulum. One is a typical globular jar form with wide mouth and medium high neck. It has an annular base, and at the base-body junction a series of flat, steplike ornaments runs all the way around the vessel at regularly spaced intervals. On the neck is attached a human-face effigy of typical Tulum style. Most of the exceedingly flaky red slip has eroded away. Curiously, the vessel lacked any signs of a floor and is reconstructed without one (fig. 15,d). The second effigy vessel, on the other side of the stairway, is a low-necked globular jar of typical Tulum Red direct rim form, with a deep ring base. Only traces of the slip, which was of medium orange color, remain. On one side of the globular body wall is attached a human-face effigy. On the other side, opposite the effigy, the vessel is drawn out into a large conical projection which almost certainly represents the east-coast caracol, a special type of large edible univalve mollusc. Running from the lower border of the caracol and sweeping upward along the vessel wall on each side are two raised ridges which join in front of the vessel to form a single peaked cap on top of the effigy head. The whole com-prises a composite monster with turtle body, human head, and caracol tail (fig. 15,i).

The multiple-mouthed jars are limited to Ichpaatun, and only four examples were noted (fig. 5,b). It is not certain whether they had two or more than two mouths. In the sherds collected two types were represented. In one type the wall of the main neck served as part of the smaller neck, the two necks thus adjoining each other and with a common wall. In the second type the smaller neck was complete in itself and separated from the main neck by 2 to 3 cm. The extra neck was always shorter than the main one and situated near the shoulder of the vessel. The two necks in the second type were connected by a horizontal strap-handle-like attachment. The smaller opening in both types lacks interior slip, whereas the large opening may or may not have slip.

In Level 2 of Trench 11 at Tulum was found part of a concave-bottom, direct rim hemispheri-cal bowl that was unique. Although only about a quarter of the vessel was recovered, it included a complete profile. In paste, original surface color, and texture it conforms closely to my Tulum Red ware. It evidently was entirely covered, except for the exterior base, with an exceedingly flaky dark brown slip (most of the interior slip has eroded away). On this slip, probably after firing, was incised in fine, shallow line a complex motif which differs markedly from the simple design on most Tulum Red ware. The design, only part restorable, is shown in figure 11,h,1. After the design was incised the background areas were covered with a thick, plaster-like, light blue paint, leaving the design in the dark brown slip color. Although not true negative painting it is a negative technique.

Supports (figs. 4; 6,a). One of the distinctive features of Tulum Red is the support. The most common type is basically tubular, hollow, and flat-bottomed. The outer side is somewhat convex in profile, and is higher than the concave inner side. Typically the outer convex side is pierced by two small round vents, aligned vertically; the lower, inner, more concave side usually has one. Some examples lack the inner vent or have only one on the outer side. In a few the vents are off-center or even placed on the lateral sides. Supports vary in maximal height from 2 to 4 cm. At Tulum there are slight variations from the basic form; only an occasional globular example occurs there with pellet rattles, and a few hollow pierced conical or small solid conical supports (fig. 6,a).

The basic type is also common at Ichpaatun and widespread along the entire north and east coast. At Ichpaatun, however, more atypical forms and far greater variety of form occur, and a much higher percentage have rattle supports; also there is more variation in the position of the vents, and pellets are commonly associated with them. In addition to other minor Tulum types found at Ichpaatun, some of the tubular supports have a concave profile both inside and out, pre-senting a spool-like cross section. A new type that occurs here is completely absent at Tulum; I am calling it the "Turkish slipper" type. It is a hollow, elongated, roughly subglobular support, the tip of which is rolled up and plastered against the side in a very flat bolster-like effect, some-what like the curled-up toe of a Turkish slipper (fig. 6,a,48,55). Also found at Ichpaatun were two very rare effigy supports, one a clownlike human face, the other an owl's head (fig. 18,e,f).

The association of support with vessel form is not entirely clear. Only one jar (fig. 5,e,4), from Tulum, had a support. It was a hollow unpierced tubular-shaped support on a vessel which in paste and finish was similar to the direct rim type but unfortunately was atypical in having a high vertical neck with bolstered rim. Without much doubt, supports are only rarely associated with jar forms. Typical pierced tubular feet and solid conical feet are associated with chile grinders; none of the more delicate incised hemispherical bowls seem to have had supports. The one bit of evidence of support associated with basal flange bowls was a hollow subglobular foot (fig. 4,c,14) having two vents on the outer side and a clay pellet inside. With the basal break bowls we are on surer ground; all of them seem to have had supports, usually of the typical tubular hollow form, never the solid or conical hollow feet. The shape affiliation of either the effigy or the Turkish slipper type is not known at all.

Bases. Basal break bowls, basal flange bowls, and hemispherical bowls all have gently convex bases. Jars are evidently associated with either flat or concave bases of greatly reduced surface area. Pedestal bases were noted with only one of the effigy vessels from Tulum (fig. 15,d); the other (fig. 15,i) has a ringstand base.

Handles. Strap handles associated with jars are rather common in Tulum Red; small loop handles, associated with the "lamp-chimney" type of exotic forms, are very rare. It is not clear whether the majority of the strap handles were placed horizontally or vertically. In only one jar, from Ichpaatun, do we have a handle attached to the body, and it is placed horizontally. The loop handles were placed vertically.

Surface

The vast bulk of the sherds show a uniform, consistent red slip which varies little either on a single vessel or from vessel to vessel. It has a medium to light polish. It tends to flake, although it is much faster than on Mayapan Red but much less tenacious than on Puuc or Chichen Red ware. On many sherds the slip is partly or completely eroded off. Colors in the Munsell (1929) color chart that run closest to the slip are in the 10R hues, especially those classed as Red 4/6 and 4/8 and Dark Red 3/6. Sherds from Ichpaatun have a more tenacious slip and somewhat higher polish.

A small but consistent percentage of Tulum Red ware in all samples runs to light-to-dark brown in slip color. The colors in the chart that are closest are in the 7.5YR hues, Strong Brown 5/6 and 5/8, and Brown 5/4. A few sherds have black or orange slips. Some clouding or color zoning occurs; it seems to have been accidental and usually is found on body sherds of large jars. Some brown-slipped vessels are probably intentional, but accidents in firing may account for others.

Basal break bowls are slipped inside and out except the bases of the supports, chile grinders in and out except the incised vessel floor. Jars, on the other hand, are not completely slipped. In the flaring rim jars the inside is slipped down only to the junction of the lower and upper segments of the neck, the entire inside of the walls being left unslipped. Bolstered rim jars are slipped on the entire outside of the vessel but on the inside of only the neck. In the direct rim jars, however, especially the smaller, thinner-walled ones, the entire vessel inside and out is slipped; in the larger ones, only the outside and inside of the neck. All jar bases are unslipped inside and out. The unslipped surfaces or eroded slip surfaces are usually a pale orange; in the coarse paste bolstered rim jars they are brick red.

Decoration

Post-slip incised (or, better, scratched) design is the only form of decoration found on Tulum Red ware except the very rare effigy vessels. The designs are repetitive and rather unimaginative, being mainly curvilinear lines enclosed in panels marked by straight lines. One distinctive feature is that most of the lines are double, even those enclosing panels. The execution is careless; the lines are scratched after the slipping and firing, and the sharp, shallow impressions just about remove the slip without cutting into the vessel. Some sherds have planorelief design areas made by scraping away the slip. The decoration runs in bands about the outside. It is found chiefly on basal break bowls and direct rim jars, and even there is uncommon. On the bowls it consists of a continuous delimited band of panels running all the way around the outside, starting from about 1 cm below the lip and extending down to 1 cm from the basal break. Round-sided bowls, not of the grinder type, may have a similar incised band just below the rim. On jars, the decoration occurs only on the direct rim type and usually on those that are slipped inside and out; it is confined to a band 3 to 6 cm wide on the neck or just below the neck-shoulder join. The decoration has never been found in association with grinders or with flaring rim jars, and only one sherd of an incised bolster rim jar was found.

Paste

Paste texture varies with vessel form. Bowls are generally to be classed as fine paste, and so are jars with the direct rim, especially the smaller and incised examples. Flaring rim and bolstered rim jars have coarser pastes running to medium coarse. Paste color is uniformly pale orange. The ware as a whole is fairly hard and breaks with a sharp, clean fracture. Technologically, in general, it is much superior to Mayapan Red and is probably about average for Mesoamerican wares as a whole. The sample from Ichpaatun again is superior technically; it seems to be harder, and it has finer pastes. A small percentage of the sherds, mainly from high-necked bolstered rim jars from Tulum, are coarse textured, softer, and more crumbly, and have a brick-red color. They are similar to red slipped sherds of Chiquila Censer ware.

As far as we could observe calcite is used as temper in this ware.

Tulum-Ichpaatun Comparisons

Throughout our description of Tulum Red we have noted a number of differences between the sample from Tulum and that from Ichpaatun. We may recapitulate them.

First, I do not think two separate wares should be defined on the basis of these minor differences; the samples from the two sites are almost identical, especially in forms.

In general the Ichpaatun sample is technically superior to that from Tulum. The ware is somewhat harder, and the slip is less flaky, is less apt to erode, and has a higher polish. I suspect also that the paste is finer, comparing form with form; certainly it is finer in the bolstered rim jars. Ichpaatun sherds show a higher incidence and greater variety of incised decoration, and more elaboration in support shapes. Leaving the general and proceeding to the particular, the following differences may be noted:

Basal Break Bowls. Rim diameter and total vessel height do not differ, but bowls from Ichpaatun are shallower and have higher supports.

Flaring Rim Jars. The over-all appearance is the same, but the Tulum jars in general have higher upper segments in proportion to the lower segments and a greater total height than the Ichpaatun jars.

Bolstered Rim Jars. Those from Tulum have coarser pastes and more rounded bolsters than those from Ichpaatun.

Exotic Forms. No effigy vessels of the type found at Tulum are known from Ichpaatun, but their scarcity at Tulum and our more intensive work there must be remembered.

Multiple-Mouthed Jars. These are completely lacking at Tulum and rare at Ichpaatun (4 examples).

Supports. Typical Tulum supports occur and are modal types at Ichpaatun, but even in the typical forms are varied with rattles, lateral and off-center vents, etc. Ichpaatun supports tend also to be taller. Moreover, we find completely new types at Ichpaatun, such as the Turkish slipper, effigy, and double-concave-sided varieties.

Decoration. Besides the greater richness and frequency of decoration we find more use of scraping and the cross hatch at Ichpaatun.

Tulum Plain Ware (fig. 6, b-e)

Tulum Plain, normally unslipped, is distinctive from all other plain wares in Quintana Roo in paste, form, and surface treatment, and serves as another diagnostic ware for the post-Classic Period. At Tulum the best sample came from Structure 35, the Cenote House, but all samples contained a high percentage of this ware. At Ichpaatun it is also important, although differing in some respects from its Tulum counterpart. Some specimens of Tulum Plain are difficult to separate from eroded Tulum Red, especially where the paste is a little finer than average. In general, however, Tulum Plain is a coarser ware.

Form. At Tulum about 90 per cent of this ware is from low-necked, wide-mouthed jars. Both bolstered and direct rims occur, with all intermediate variations; in fact, all Tulum Red jar neck and rim forms except the flaring rim are duplicated in Tulum Plain. The ware is obviously closely related to Tulum Red and part of a single ceramic tradition. Neck heights vary from 2 to 6 cm, most of the rims running between 3 and 5 cm. In the few specimens whose rim diameters could be calculated the following measurements were recorded: 30, 35, 26, 31, 40, 28, 29, 24, and 33 cm. Most of the rims seem to have come from vessels of about the height and shape of the Tulum Red direct rim jars. Actually no restorable vessels were found, only a few bases, and our shape analysis is little more than a calculated guess. Two types of handles occur with this ware: small, vertical flat loop handles, running from just below the lip to a point a few centimeters below the shoulder-neck junction; and the standard strap placed horizontally just below the shoulder. In some vessels lugs also occur at the shoulder-neck junction. The smaller loop handles usually go with small vessels.

At Ichpaatun, the ware, the jar shapes, and the sizes largely duplicate those from Tulum. One difference is the higher frequency of miniature and generally small vessels at Ichpaatun. Rim diameters from Ichpaatun were 34, 34, 36, 27, 40, 40, and 14 cm.

Ichpaatun collections differ markedly from Tulum samples in having a large number of hemispherical bowls and even plates and comals. At Tulum only the bowls are found, and they are exceedingly rare. Some of the comals and plates have loop handles placed horizontally on the rims, and at both Ichpaatun and Tulum bowls often have flat lugs or horizontal handles on or just below the rim. Two bowls from Ichpaatun had rim diameters of 15 and 25 cm; three plates or comals had diameters of 22, 31, and 38 cm.

Surface. The surface is unslipped, smoothed, but not usually burnished or polished. The degree of smoothing varies greatly. The absence of striations is one of the features that distinguish this from many Yucatecan plain wares. Color variation is considerable, and firing in general appears to have been carelessly done with little care in its control. Sherds vary in color from a yellow buff to dirty buff, pale orange, brick red, and smoky black. Buff occurs in much the highest percentage and perhaps may be considered the type color. The Ichpaatun ware is technically superior, with better-controlled firing, and most sherds are a gray-buff color.

Paste. A few of the smaller vessels show fine-textured pastes, but in general the paste ranges from medium coarse to coarse. The ware seems to be calcite-tempered, is moderately hard and brittle, and breaks with sharp, well defined fracture edges. Paste color varies through the range noted for the surface and is generally uneven.

Fine Orange (fig. 7,a)

Fine orange ware, though exceedingly rare in Quintana Roo, has great spatial range. Most of our type sherds are from Tulum, partly because Tulum was one of the few sites intensively excavated. Sherds of fine orange were found at Yuukluuk, Cancun, El Meco, Vista Alegre, San Miguel, Mulchi, El Diez, and Tancah. Very curious and perhaps statistically significant is the lack of it at Ichpaatun. The heaviest concentrations occurred at Tulum, Mulchi, and El Meco.

A comparison of the material from Quintana Roo with that from other areas is hampered by the poor state of preservation and the small size of many of the sherds. In the Merida collections of Carnegie Institution are samples of fine orange pottery from numerous Yucatecan sites which were gathered in part by Brainerd and from which he defined his primary Z and X types. Neither of these types was found in Quintana Roo. In the Mayapan samples at the same office are a small but consistent number of fine orange sherds which are very close to our Quintana Roo samples and are different from Brainerd's X and Z. In a recent publication Berlin (1956) has labeled this type of fine orange "V" and dates it as Late post-Classic. He also defines a U Fine Orange which evidently is immediately pre-Conquest. All my fine orange sherds from the east coast that are in condition to be classified conform to Berlin's type V and presumably are imports. As I was able to examine Berlin's collections the identification is certain.

The variation in shape is considerable, especially when the small size of my sample is taken into account. Basal break and round-sided bowls are frequent, some having medial moldings or lateral ridges. Two rims found at Tulum seem to come from very tall vertical-walled vessels. One sherd from Tulum is a miniature vessel with pedestal support. It may well be U Fine Orange, since Berlin lists such a support specifically as a U and not a V Fine Orange trait. Slab supports, however, his major diagnostic for U, were not found. Supports were either effigy (virtually identical with Berlin's examples; see his fig. 10),or hollow bulbous rattle—both typical V forms. Vessels with lateral ridges, or, as Berlin calls them, medial moldings, are both U and V forms.

Decoration in my Quintana Roo sample was simple geometric fine-line incision with a few painted sherds from El Meco. Designs are very close to those published by Berlin (1956, figs. 5,rrr; 6,b,c) as V Fine Orange.

Mayapan Black-on-Cream (fig. 7,b)

The samples of this ware from Quintana Roo sites are identical in form and surface treatment to samples from Mayapan. The ware enjoys a wide geographical range in Quintana Roo, although it is nowhere an important one. Our type sample is from Tulum and Ichpaatun, but the ware occurs also at Tancah, Vista Alegre, Aguada Grande, Mulchi, and Monte Bravo.

Form. With few exceptions all the sherds are from bolstered rim high-to-medium-necked jars. One of our type rims is similar in form to that of Yucatan Slate basins. Strap handles are common, in one vessel placed horizontally on the basin rim. Flat and concave bases go with this ware.

Surface. These vessels are usually completely slipped on the outside except for the base; on the inside, jars are slipped on the necks only. The slip color ranges from dead white to creamy to pale yellow, pale orange, and even rosy, but most sherds are whitish. Usually the whiter slips go with the lighter paste and surface colors, the rosy and pale orange with brick-red pastes. The slip is always only lightly polished and extremely flaky.

Decoration. Decoration consists of crudely painted dead black or dark brown parallel vertical bands, of uneven spacing and width, either on the inside or outside of the neck and often running down the shoulder of the vessel.

Paste. Sherds can be sorted into two sharply divergent groups. One has a strong orange to brick-red paste and is coarse grained and brittle; the other is buff to yellow in paste color, medium coarse in texture, and more crumbly. The basin rim is of fine-textured paste. I do not know the vertical or horizontal significance of these differences. An occasional sherd of this ware is difficult to distinguish from Yucatan Black on Slate, especially if the sherd was found in salt-saturated beach sand and only traces of the original slip remain. In general, Black on Slate has a finer paste.

Censer Wares (figs. 7,c,d; 8; 15,f,h; 16; 17; 18)

One of the major problems in east-coast ceramics is establishing the distinctions and the mutual relations between the various types of censer ware that date from the post-Classic period. Although all these wares, from Chiquila to Ichpaatun, have a fundamental similarity in form, there are important regional differences in paste and surface treatment. All of them closely resemble in style the censer ware from Mayapan and reflect an over-all unity in religious concepts and ritualistic techniques for the period. A typical form found in Mayapan and all along the east coast, irrespective of local variations in the ware, is a tall pedestal base jar or vase-like vessel to which is attached a full-length figurine dressed in elaborate costume and with winglike back ornaments, plumes, pendants, and fans. They evidently were painted with a thick, heavy, plaster-like paint that rarely survives the erosive effects of deposition, blue, white, and yellow being favorite colors. No complete vessel of this type could be reconstructed, but the sherds indicate a close similarity in form to the reconstructed examples from Mayapan. Although the bulk of our censer sherds are from vessels of this type, a few come from other forms, and they will be described separately under our ware designations. The following types were defined tentatively.

Chiquila Censer (figs. 7,c; 15,f; 16,b,c,e,o; 17,1,n,q,w,y; 18,a-d). Chiquila Censer ware is mainly a north-coast variant, being restricted in our samples almost entirely to coastal sites, and it occurs only sporadically south of Mulchi. It is especially common at such sites as Chiquila, the type site, Yuukluuk, Cancun, El Meco, and Cocal 1 and 2. Most of it is unslipped, but a consistent small proportion carries a red, brown, or orange slip similar to that found on Tulum Red; it is the only censer type that does carry a slip. The vast bulk of the sherds, however, are unslipped and of a pale-to-medium orange color which in the salty beach sand turns to a brick red. The paste runs from strong orange to brick red, generally the latter, and is sharply differentiated from Tulum Buff Paste Censer ware by its hardness and greater coarseness and in having an abundance of large angular particles of temper. It is much more brittle, and breaks with a cleaner fracture, than Tulum Buff Paste Censer, in this respect resembling Tulum Plain more than Buff Paste Censer ware.

This type is distinctive not only in slipping but also in the more frequent use of incision as a decorative technique on the walls of the vessel, and in the technique of piercing the walls, cutting out triangles or diamonds to form a decorative pattern in conjunction with the incision. Some of the incision is fine line, some is deeply grooved.

A typical design technique in this as well as in other Quintana Roo censer types is the application of a thick ribbon of clay around the vessel, just above the junction of body with annular base, into which a series of parallel vertical grooves is pressed, probably with the fingernail.

Chiquila Censer ware differs sharply from Mayapan censers in having large female, rather than male, figurines attached to the vessel. The figurines wear triangular embroidered or rectangular plain collars with the breasts left uncovered. Except for this variation, the vessel form and the figurine are almost identical to those of the Mayapan effigy censers, including specific forms of plumes, fans, buttons, and rectangular back ornaments or wings.

One complete vessel of Chiquila Censer ware recovered from El Meco serves as a good model for shape in this ware, although the figurine was absent (fig. 15,f). The vessel stands about 26 cm high, the pedestal base accounting for 7.5 cm. The base is pierced, and the floor is blackened by incense burning. The walls are nearly vertical. The vessel falls into our vasiform type with a small, flat, bolstered rim; it is incised, and the walls are pierced by diamond and triangular perforations in four vertical panels, each separated by undecorated areas with a button applied. There are traces of red slip on the surface.

The vessels accompanied by figurines were evidently considerably larger than the one just described. A vessel from Chiquila, which has a heavy, bolstered rim and globular jarlike body, stands 21 cm high from lip to the base of the breast of the attached figurine (fig. 18,a). Another, which has a leg attached to the pedestal base, has a base height of 16 cm.

Rims in general are bolstered; pedestal base rims may or may not have bolsters. In spite of our large type sample from Chiquila very few human faces, or parts of faces, were recovered. Only one complete face, unfortunately not a female but a male with huge projecting fangs, was found. From Yuukluuk another part of a face was recovered which may go with a female figure. One alligator effigy was found at Chiquila (fig. 17,y). Its vessel affiliation is uncertain; it may be a ladle handle. An interesting specimen from Chiquila (fig. 16,c) is a beautifully modeled human hand holding a bowl of copal. Here again the similarity to Mayapan censer ware is close.

Tulum Buff Paste Censer (figs. 7,d; 8,a,b,30; 15,h; 16,h,m,n,p-w; 17,a,e,m,r). South of Mulchi and Puerto Morelos, Tulum Buff Paste Censer ware replaces Chiquila Censer ware, to which it is closely allied. Our type sample is from Tulum, where it reaches high frequencies in some of the trenches.

Tulum Buff Paste Censer differs from Chiquila Censer ware principally in the color of paste and surface, which is commonly shades of buff. In general the core of the paste is somewhat darker, running to medium and dark gray, and the outer paste and surface range from yellow to pale orange buff. This type lacks the high percentage of temper inclusions characteristic of Chiquila Censer, is much more crumbly, and is softer. Incision is rare as a decorative technique, but the fingernail-impressed appliqué ribbon is common. Slipping is absent, if our sample can be considered definitive. Many sherds show traces of a thick, heavy, plaster-like paint, usually white, less commonly blue. Rims are generally bolstered, pedestal base rims may or may not be, and over-all shapes are similar to those of Chiquila Censer ware.

All the identifiable figurine parts from Tulum are from males, and some seven complete or partial human faces were recovered. Most of them portray a single individual with two big projecting fangs and a savage, warlike countenance (fig. 17,a-e). They are very similar in style to those from Mayapan. Two are complete and evidently did not go with bodies but were attached to vessel walls as in the two effigy vessels of Tulum Red ware. One of the latter portrays the same individual.

Ornaments from the figurines duplicate those from Chiquila even in minor details.

Besides the forms common to these two censer wares we find two new ones in Tulum Buff Paste Censer that are duplicated at Mayapan, although there they are not censers. One is a small, cuplike vessel with three solid peglike feet, which stands 7.3 cm high and has a rim diameter of 6 cm (figs. 8,b,30; 15,h). The second is another cuplike vessel in the form of a rabbit effigy (fig. 8,a,10). It has a pedestal base; its total height is 8.8 cm, and its rim diameter 7.3 cm. Neither is from Tulum; the first is from a superficial deposit at Tancah, the second from Ak 1.

Aguada Grande Censer (figs. 8,e; 18,g-j). From the site of Aguada Grande were recovered approximately 2000 sherds of a curious type of censer which bears little similarity in shape to any of our other post-Classic censer types but which resembles Tulum Black Paste Censer in at least surface and paste features. The ware is technically very poor, extremely crumbly and soft. Most of the sherds disintegrated at the edges in being transported from Cozumel to Merida, so that complete vessel restoration was impossible. The surface is smoothed but unslipped, and is generally a pale orange-brown or orange-buff. The paste runs to very dark colors, often black.

All the sherds seem to come from a single vessel form: a tall cone-shaped type with a vented pedestal base. Above the base the vessel flares gradually outward to reach a maximum width at the mouth. Two partly restorable examples were recovered, each having a total height of 19 cm and a mouth diameter of 18.1 cm (fig. 18,i,j). Lips of the rim and of the pedestal base are unbolstered. The characteristic feature of the form, however, lies in the modeling. Instead of attaching a figurine face or full figure the potter constructed the vessel itself in the form of a very crude human face on which modeled additions to represent eyes, nose, and mouth were applied, and the pupils, nostrils, and mouth opening were pierced. Evidently, when incense was burnt, smoke filtered out through these openings. As in the Ehecatl drawings in the Aztec codices, the mouth is sharply projecting and pursed; sometimes it is open, with two projecting fangs or filled with a whole row of them; in one vessel the tongue hangs out. Noses vary from sharp, narrow, hooklike forms to grotesques. The eye is modeled by piercing a hole for the pupil, then surrounding it with a roll of clay, and finally adding rolls above and below for the lids. Characteristic decorations include one or two rows of what are evidently meant to represent tubular beads attached vertically on the vessel below the effigy mouth. The total effect is grotesque.

This type represents, I believe, the final phase of censer-making on the east coast. The facts that it occurs on floors of structures at Aguada Grande, that it is restricted to the site, and that Cozumel was one of the few places occupied in post-Conquest times all suggest that the type may even be Colonial in date. Aguada Grande, with its position on the northernmost tip of the island, far from San Miguel, the center of Spanish conversion activities, may well have been one of the last strongholds of paganism in Yucatan. The argument is strengthened by the probable technical affiliation with the following type.

Tulum Black Paste Censer (figs. 8,d; 16,g,i-l; 17,j,k). Most of the sites on Cozumel Island along with Kilometer 35 on the mainland directly across from Cozumel yielded a consistent percentage of sherds almost identical in paste and surface to Aguada Grande Censer ware. The bodies, however, were different in shape, and the grotesque modeling was absent. Instead, typical Tulum and Chiquila modeling correlates with this ware. It was not until the 1955 season that the chronological position of Tulum Black Paste Censer ware became established. It occurs at Tulum on the floors of Structures 2 and 4 and certainly represents the final phase of censer-ware manufacturing at that site. As it is almost identical in paste and surface to Aguada Grande Censer ware, the latter was probably derived from it. It evidently was a widespread type along the coast from Tulum to Kilometer 35 and on Cozumel Island, and probably represents the last pre-Conquest ceramic phase of east-coast chronology. Presumably this was the type used when Cozumel was still functioning as a great pilgrimage center for northern Yucatan.

The major difference between this type and that from Aguada Grande is shape. One restorable vessel from Tulum (fig. 8,d,1) and a large sherd from Celerain 1 are alike in having high vertical walls with a slightly outflaring neck, and a direct rim and globular body. The Tulum vessel has a pedestal base with a direct rim. Bolstered rims are rare, but a pedestal base from Tulum has one. From Kilometer 35 was collected a small vessel of this type which duplicates the little tripod vessel of Tulum Buff Paste Censer previously described. It shows relationship, moreover, with Tulum Buff Paste Censer and Chiquila Censer in the use of the appliqued-band fingernail-punched design and the full figurine attached to the vessel. One shark figurine of this ware was collected at Ak 1 (fig. 8,d,8).

Ichpaatun Censer (figs. 8,b; 16,a,b,i; 17,f-h,o,p,s,u). This type is almost identical with Tulum Buff Paste Censer, the chief differences being that it is much harder, breaks with a cleaner fracture, runs to gray buff rather than yellow buff, and has much more temper in the paste. At Ichpaatun body sherds of this ware are almost impossible to distinguish from the local variety of Tulum Plain. Only shape differences separate the two types, and shapes are very similar to those of Tulum Buff Paste Censer; even the figurine faces are identical. A novelty at Ichpaatun is the use of this ware for making human-effigy whistles.

Ladle Censers (figs. 8,c; 17,o-r). These are rather rare on the east coast but are widely distributed. Complete examples of Tulum Censer, Chiquila Censer, and Ichpaatun Censer types were found at Tulum, Tancah, Kilometer 14, Yuukluuk, Chiquila, and Ichpaatun. There is a remarkable similarity in form in the examples spread over this huge area. All are simple, hollow, tubular handles with open ends. At Ichpaatun one dog effigy handle was found, and the only bowl sherd definitely to go with a handle came from the same site.

VISTA ALEGRE-SAN MIGUEL COMPLEX WARES

Vista Alegre Striated (fig. 9,a)

Vista Alegre Striated is one of the most distinctive of Yucatecan plain wares; it is easily differentiated from all other striated wares on the basis of shape. Its chronological position is uncertain, but I believe it to be in the Early Mexican period. With Yucatan Slate it makes up a ceramic complex that dominates the samples from Vista Alegre and San Miguel. The ware is also found at Kilometer 14, Solfarino, Monte Bravo, Chiquila, Leona Vicario, Aguada Grande, El Meco, San Gervasio, and very rarely at Tancah. Its great range and distinctiveness will make it an excellent time marker once it is securely dated. At Tancah it definitely is late in the history of the site but earlier than the Tulum Period; Tancah, however, is the only site where it is stratigraphically placed.

Form. The ware comes in two forms: (a) restricted orifice bowls with flat bottoms, direct or thickened rims without bolsters, and vertical strap handles which join in general about 2 cm below the lip; (b) high vertical-necked jars with direct or slightly bolstered rims. Most examples of (b) are limited to Vista Alegre and possibly to San Miguel.

Surface. The basal surface is uniformly pale yellow-buff or pale orange-buff, smoothed but unburnished. Sherds are striated on the exterior sides only. Striations are shallow but well cut. On restricted orifice bowls they may be a narrow band of horizontal parallel lines on the exterior of the lip, starting from the point where it curves inward at a sharp angle, or, if the rim curves gradually in from the wall, striations may run from lip to base or start about 2 cm from the rim and cover the wall of the vessel. In the bowls with sharp-angle incurve there may be an upper zone of horizontal striations running from the lip down for 2 cm or so and then, running into it, diagonal striations that evidently covered the rest of the vessel. In jars, striations are on the neck beginning 0.5 cm below the lip and running vertically. Some sherds show two striation zones, a horizontal one on the upper part of the neck and a diagonal one on the lower. It is not known whether jar bodies were striated as well. All bases recovered are flat and are striated even on the bottom exterior.

Paste. In paste the ware shows more variation than in surface treatment. The Vista Alegre sample has in general a fine-textured paste; at San Miguel it runs to medium coarse. Paste color is pale orange to brick red, the red being especially common at San Miguel. In general the ware is rather soft and crumbly.

Yucatan Slate Ware (fig. 11,a,1-4,22-49)

Yucatan Slate, defined by Brainerd as Yucatan Medium Slate, is one of the basic wares of the State of Yucatan for the Classic Period (Regional and Florescent). In a previous discussion we have pointed out the chronological problems it presents. In the Territory of Quintana Roo it is definitely Classic; it replaces Tancah Variegated and Tancah Red as the main slipped ware at Tancah, and throughout Quintana Roo it is a common ware, especially in Late Classic times, possibly persisting as an important ware into the early post-Classic period. Although closely allied to its Yucatecan counterpart it gives the impression in the Territory of being locally made, and at a number of separate centers, for paste varies markedly from site to site. Forms, however, are limited to a very few standard types found all over the area. The best samples were collected at Tancah, San Miguel, and Vista Alegre, but the ware is also common at Kilometer 14 and El Diez, and a few sherds were found at Calderitas, El Cedral, Xelha, Aguada Grande, and Monte Bravo. The following analysis is based principally upon the Tancah, San Miguel, and Vista Alegre samples.

Form. Most of the sherds are from three basic forms: (1) Heavy bolstered rim basins, of which most fall into Brainerd's Puuc Convex Interior type with a few Chenes Concave Interior rims. These vessels have large vertical strap handles. (2) Basal break tripod bowls with solid slab supports. These vessels have interiorly flattened lips and are extremely regular in form over the huge region of northern Quintana Roo. They are exactly the same as Brainerd's Yucatecan type 4, which he states has an eastern distribution in the State. Four restorable vessels were found of this form (fig. 11,a,1-4), one from El Diez, one from Tancah, and two from Kilometer 14. (3) Jars having vertical stripes of red, dark brown, or rarely black painted over the slate slip.

Surface. All vessels of this ware carry an over-all slip, waxy, translucent, and very fast, with few sherds showing flaking. The ware frequently shows crazing. Color of the slip varies considerably, showing yellowish to reddish brown and even lavendar tints, but generally running to flat browns and grays. The slip is the most distinctive feature, contrasting sharply with the flakier, more matte slips of other Classic Yucatecan wares.

Decoration. Some of the basal break bowls have two parallel lines of fingernail impressions placed horizontally on the exterior just above the basal break. Some of the jars and even the basins have stripes painted vertically on the exterior.

<u>Paste</u>. Pastes in general must be classed as fine-textured with a small percentage of medium coarse. The ware is harder than most Yucatecan wares, and it fractures with a sharp, clean, even break. Paste color varies considerably, ranging from pale orange to olive brown, running generally to red and buff.

Yucatecan Thin Slate (fig. 11,<u>a</u>,5-21)

In his survey of Yucatecan ceramics Brainerd set up a general ware or group of wares under the heading Yucatan Slate. One of the types has already been described and labeled Medium Slate. Another type, with the same slip characteristics as Medium Slate, he called Thin Slate. In the laboratory study of my Quintana Roo material I followed Brainerd's classification, and, as there was no chronological difference between Medium and Thin Slate either in Yucatan or Quintana Roo, I frequently counted sherds of the two together. Smith, in a reappraisal of all northern Yucatecan ceramics, to be published later, states that in paste and form the distinctions between the two are strong enough to set up a separate ware classification. Here, therefore, to avoid later confusion, I am describing Thin Slate independently, even though my sherd counts in general do not separate the two.

<u>Form</u>. Thin Slate is technically and aesthetically the finest ware in Quintana Roo. In vessels 10 cm high, the walls are characteristically very thin, running from 3 to 5 mm, on the average. Vessels found in Quintana Roo have slightly convex or flat bases. Two basic forms occur in the Territory. One is a deep bowl with straight, almost vertical, walls, basal break, slightly convex base, and usually a rim with a flat rectangular exterior molding running around the lip. It often has a basal molding of the same type. Sometimes the rim is slightly incurving. A second type is the hemispherical bowl with direct rim and no moldings.

<u>Surface</u>. The same as Medium Slate, but almost all the sherds run to light brown or yellow-brown.

<u>Decoration</u>. Besides the already-mentioned use of basal and lip moldings as decorative elements, one restorable vessel of Thin Slate had a band of post-firing, carved geometric design (fig. 11,<u>a</u>,6).

<u>Paste</u>. The paste is finer than that of Medium Slate or what we are here calling Yucatan Slate. It is fine to very fine in texture. The color range, with the exception of red, which is mainly absent, is about the same as that of Yucatan Slate, and general technical excellence is about the same.

TANCAH COMPLEX WARES

Late Formative Monochrome

Within this ware I have classified three types which I am calling Tancah Red, Tancah Variegated, and Chiquila Variegated. In paste, form, and decoration Tancah Red and Tancah Variegated are identical. The only distinction between the two lies in slip color, red in Tancah Red and exceedingly variable in Variegated, several slip colors often being combined on a single vessel. The distinction is important chronologically, and therefore throughout the text I have separated the two types. In form, slip variation, and decoration Tancah Red and Tancah Variegated are very close to R. E. Smith's (1955) Chicanel and Brainerd's (1951) Late Formative Slipped ware of the State of Yucatan. A few sherds of Tancah Red seem to show resemblances to Coba Red (a Regional Period ware) in rim form, and Brainerd points out that his Late Formative Red Slipped from northern Yucatan and his various Regional Red Slipped wares are similar in all but rim form and constitute a single tradition. Chiquila Variegated, which has a northern distribution in Quintana Roo as opposed to Tancah Variegated with its central Quintana Roo distribution, is identical with the latter in paste, slip, and decoration, but the rim forms are closer to those of the Regional wares. The relative chronological position of these three types is a difficult problem, which is discussed in full in the text. The types are described separately below.

Tancah Red (figs. 9,b; 15,j)

Outside the type site, this type is rare in our samples, occurring sporadically and in small percentages. Its closest ties are with Mani Monochrome (a variant of Brainerd's Late Formative Red Slipped ware) from Yucatan.

Form. Most sherds are either from hemispherical bowls or from deep, vertical straight-sided basal break bowls with flat bottoms. The following forms occur in this type. (1) Deep vertical or nearly vertical walled basal break bowls with flat bases. Rims in this form are of several types: sharply everted rims with a rectangular, bullet, or beak-like cross section, or concavo-convex. (2) Subglobular bowls with rounded bolstered rims and flat bases. (3) Hemispherical bowls. (4) Vase-like vessels with vertical walls and lateral ridges just below the lips. (5) Jars with a low neck and flaring rim, and jars with a high vertical neck. Jars in general are rare. (6) A number of sherds may be from comals or plates. Deep vertical-sided bowls with flat bases and everted lips dominate this ware. Supports and in general handles are lacking except for one restorable vessel which had three vertical handles (fig. 9,b,1).

Surface. The ware is defined on the basis of its red slip; the 10R hues 4/8 and 4/6 come closest, varying to orange and reddish brown. The color is similar to Tulum Red but is duller and more matte. The slip is fragile, often flaked off, and has a light polish, which increases in the thinner-walled, finer vessels. In the bowl and vase forms, slip is applied over the entire vessel except the base exterior. In low-necked jars the entire exterior except the base is slipped, but only the neck in the interior. High-necked forms may carry no interior slip. The base color of the unslipped surface is similar to paste colors.

Decoration. Only about 4 per cent of the sherds from our Tancah type collection have decoration other than slipping; it consists of fine to medium straight-line incision. Designs are simple parallel straight or curving lines which run around the vessel in bands beginning just below the lip and often continuing to the basal break. The designs are not paneled, but continuous.

Paste. Paste in general runs to pale orange and brick red, with individual sherds covering the range in between. It is tempered with angular white and gray particles, probably sherd or calcite in origin. In general the ware runs to fine-textured paste, with some temper, and is only moderately hard.

Tancah Variegated (figs. 9c; 10,a)

In all respects except surface treatment, Tancah Variegated is identical to Tancah Red and is probably derived from it. It is much more common in our over-all samples than Tancah Red.

Form. The forms described for Tancah Red are found in this type in the same relative proportion.

Surface. Our definition of Tancah Variegated as a separate type from Tancah Red is based mainly on differences in slipping and decoration. In general it might be said that Tancah Variegated is a developmental stage of Tancah Red in which new colors are added to the basic red-orange and red-brown, and in which incised decoration is more important as a decorative technique. At Tancah the two run almost concurrently, but Tancah Red persists later and it occurs in greater numerical strength in the earliest period. Besides red, sherds are slipped in dark, medium, and light brown, black, yellow, white, orange, oyster gray, dark gray, lavendar, cream, yellow-brown, and orange-brown, but reds, browns, black, and gray predominate. The lighter colors tend to show trickle and have the waxy luster of Yucatan Slate (grays, cream, yellow); the darker colors are more matte. Mottling is common, some very pleasing aesthetic effects being achieved by this technique. Two colors are usually applied, one on the outside, one inside the vessel, or an over-all slip with a second color is painted over the sherd in a zonal relationship to incised and punctate decoration. Sometimes an interior slip is extended to cover the exterior lip; at times this is reversed, or the slips meet evenly at the top of the lip. In vessels with everted lips the everted surface may be slipped one color and the rest of the vessel, exterior and interior, another color. A few sherds are slipped entirely in one color.

The color-chart symbols that approximate closest to the color scheme of Tancah Variegated are as follows: Red 10R 4/8, 4/6; Yellowish Brown 10YR 5/6, 5/8; Strong Brown 7.5YR 5/6, 5/8; Dark Brown 7.5YR 4/4; Pink 7.5YR 8/4; Light Gray 10YR 7/2; Yellow Red 5YR 4/6, 4/8; Very Pale Brown 10YR 7/3; Reddish Gray 10R 6/1; Black 7.5R N2/.

Decoration. Decoration is much more common than in Tancah Red. Five out of seven of our test sherds have some form of incised or punctated decoration. Incision contrasts sharply with that on Tulum Red ware and might better be called grooved. Deep, wide lines that excavate well into the clay body of the vessel were evidently made with a blunt tool after slipping and before firing. A small amount of finer incision is present on the thinner-walled pieces. Round and wedge-like punctates often accompany the design. Designs are geometric, consisting of straight lines forming steps or enclosed rectangles, zigzags, and parallel lines, accompanied by rows of punctates. Curvilinear motifs are rare. Usually the designs cover the exterior vertical wall of the vessel from just below the rim to the basal break, or they may be made on top of the everted lip. A simple type consists of a single grooved line, or two or three of them, running horizontally around the vessel. Incision and punctating are often combined with zoned slipping over the base slip to give a pleasing contrast in colored rectangles enclosed by grooves, but the coincidence is not always consistent and sometimes the applied slip color may be enclosed by grooved lines but then spill over for 1 to 2 cm outside of them. One complete incised vessel was recovered (fig. 9,c,2); it shows the basic character of decoration in this ware very well.

Paste. Apparently identical to Tancah Red.

Chiquila Variegated (fig. 10,b)

The sample from Kantunil Kin, Chiquila, and other northern sites conforms closely in paste and surface treatment to our Tancah sample but diverges in rim form. I have tentatively separated these sherds in my seriation charts as Chiquila Variegated. Strictly speaking, Tancah Variegated does not occur north of Puerto Morelos. The two may possibly turn out to differ in chronological distribution, with Tancah Variegated earlier and tending to a Formative date, Chiquila later and Early Classic.

Tancah Plain — Tancah Striated (fig. 10,c-f)

One of the most difficult unsolved problems of east-coast ceramics is the relationship of Tancah Plain and Tancah Striated. I am not sure they are not the same ware, with some sherds coming from unstriated areas of the same vessels from which striated sherds derive. Although the wares are abundant in our Tancah samples, sherds in general were small and many rims cannot definitely be connected with vessel shapes. Striated sherds, moreover, are often badly weathered and difficult to classify. In a personal communication Robert Smith states that a sizable percentage of the sherds classed as either Tancah Plain or Tancah Striated are probably weathered Regional Period red-slipped types which generally are similar in paste and have flaky, poorly preserved slips. This would check with the apparent long life of the two wares as indicated in the skew frequency charts from Tancah.

I am unsatisfied with this category, and the following analysis must be accepted with caution.

Form. No differences in lip and vessel form can definitely be pointed out between Tancah Plain and Tancah Striated. Most of the jars seem to have had thick globular, rectangular, or trianguloid rims; a few had direct rims, and a few basal break bowls of the form found in Tancah Red and Tancah Variegated had everted rims. Associated with both Striated and Plain is a highly distinctive type of support. These supports are round and generally large, as the drawings in figure 10,d indicate. They usually are partly hollow with a solid lower part, more rarely solid throughout, and have a flat or round bottom with sharply flaring sides. They occur at most of the sites where the wares were identified. Most of the examples from Tancah are flat-bottomed; those from farther north tend toward rounded bottoms.

Paste and Surface. Paste in both wares is medium to coarse in texture, soft, granular and crumbly, and highly variable as to color, running from pale orange to buff, sometimes with dark gray or black cores, or even brick red. I have a note to the effect that striated sherds tend more to buff colors and dark cores, unstriated to orange and brick red, but I am not sure that the sorting is consistent. Surfaces are smoothed but unslipped and unpolished, when eroded have a grainy sandy touch, and range in color from buff to pale orange with some sherds running to red, smoky, and strong orange colors. Again I noted that striated sherds tend to buff colors, unstriated to orange and red.

Decoration. Tancah Striated is characterized by raked or striated designs. The depth of the striation varies from deep to very faint, and generally consists of parallel lines running vertically, horizontally, or diagonally with respect to the vessel. As so few large sherds were collected it is not certain how much of the vessel was striated. Certainly part at least of the body and the neck of jars had this decoration, which usually stopped 1 to 2 cm from the lip but sometimes ran to the lip. Sherds classed as Tancah Plain lack striations and may be a distinct ware or may simply come from vessels that did not have over-all striation. The ware shows close relationships to Calderitas Striated and less close to Vista Alegre Striated.

Restricted Orifice Bowls (fig. 10,c). When rims of this sort were first noted at Tancah I identified them as Vista Alegre Striated, which differs from Tancah Striated mainly in form. Later study established the further distinction that the Tancah examples have bolstered rims. Moreover, at Tancah handles are more common and spring from the top of the bolstered rim or from some point on the bolster. In Vista Alegre Striated they are less common and are usually attached well below the rim. It was further noted that this new restricted orifice bowl form, although occurring in association with the typical Yucatan Slate-Vista Alegre assemblage, was sometimes associated with earlier ceramic complexes, as at Kantunil Kin, where it goes with Regional Polychrome basal flange bowls and Chiquila Variegated. It presumably is earlier in first appearance than Vista Alegre Striated and may have served as its prototype. The shape is affiliated very closely with Tancah Plain and Tancah Striated and may be considered a variant form of those wares.

REGIONAL POLYCHROME (figs. 10,g; 15,k,l)

Although a relatively minor ware, Regional Polychrome has an enormous distribution in eastern and northern Yucatan. Defined by Brainerd previously from collections made in the State of Yucatan, it occurs over the entire Territory of Quintana Roo. The best samples collected are from Kantunil Kin and Tancah, but it occurs also at Vista Alegre, Chiquila, San Miguel, Aguada Grande, and Calderitas. Brainerd's original definition of the ware was more specific than the one used here, being restricted to pottery closely allied to the Polychrome of the Tzakol Period in the Peten (Smith, 1955). At the time that the Quintana Roo samples were analyzed in the laboratory Smith's definitive report on Uaxactun ceramics (ibid.) with his complex classification of Peten wares had not been published. Most of my material correlated very closely with Brainerd's Regional Polychrome, but some of it seemed not to be typical Tzakol in form but closer to early Tepeu, and among the Quintana Roo samples were a number of monochrome sherds. All these sherds were similar in paste and slip color and were included under Brainerd's designation Regional Polychrome. Since the samples were studied Smith's report has been published, and checking through his classification revealed that all the Quintana Roo samples can be included in his broad ware designation Peten Gloss. In the ware descriptions in our earlier discussion of Regional Polychrome (see p. 232 above), comparisons with his specific kinds of Peten Gloss are made.

In Quintana Roo, Regional Polychrome appears first at the end of the Tancah Complex and is in common association with Yucatan Slate and other San Miguel Complex wares. The outstanding trait of this ware is its amazing uniformity of paste and surface treatment over the Territory. The following description is based on the large samples from Tancah and Kantunil Kin. The Kantunil Kin sample consists mostly of Tzakol basal flange bowls; that from Tancah covers the entire time span of the ware.

Form. Regional Polychrome is one of the most complex of wares in terms of form elaboration. Five general classes may be defined: (a) Typical Tzakol basal flange bowls; probably the ring bases go with this form. (b) Simple bowls with rounded or flat bases; one complete vessel and one restorable vessel go with this shape (fig. 15,k). The complete vessel is monochrome with a red slip. (c) Tall vertical-walled forms closely allied to those of the Tepeu Period in the Peten. (d) Lateral-ridged bowls or dishes. (e) Rare forms of which the three restorable vessels (figs. 10,g,1,33; 15,l) are unique examples. One was found inverted over the skull and shoulders of a burial at Tancah (see page 165 and fig. 15,l). This vessel, using Smith's classification system, is called a Tzakol Z Angle Monochrome Bowl.

Surface. Base color is a pale, pastel-like shade of orange, uniform in individual sherds and from sherd to sherd. It is unburnished but well smoothed. All vessels are at least partly slipped with a very fragile rich orange, red, reddish brown, or, rarely, white or black slip. Normally slips are orange and red, one applied to the interior, the other to the exterior, of the vessel. Lips may often be painted black or brown exteriorly and interiorly over the slip for 1 cm or so down each side in a continuous band. Basal flange bowls are completely slipped interiorly, and exteriorly slipped down to and including the upper surface of the flange. Lateral-ridged bowls are slipped over the entire interior and the exterior as far as the ridge. Simple bowls and deep vases are completely slipped.

Most of the sherds also carry geometric designs, both angular and curvilinear, in red and black on one of the two surfaces, dependent on the form. Designs are usually in solid red areas bordered by thick black, sometimes dark brown, lines. In the basal flange bowl form the design is usually in red and black on an interior orange slip or black on an interior red slip, more commonly the former. In a few rare examples basal flange bowls may have exterior design. Exceptions to this rule are simple parallel banding in red, black, and orange on the exterior wall and painting of the exterior face of the basal flange. Decoration in the lateral-ridged bowl form occurs generally in the form of parallel stripes of red and orange paint on the exterior above the ridges. Deep vases have exterior design, and simple bowls in general are monochrome.

Paste. Regional Polychrome is tempered with black angular particles, and temper content is high. The paste in general is a dull, pale brick red, ranging in texture from medium coarse to medium fine in the basal flange bowls. Lateral ridged and tall vase forms have finer pastes, some being classifiable as fine textured. The ware is only of moderate hardness.

CHETUMAL AREA CLASSIC WARES

Calderitas Striated (fig. 11,b)

Calderitas Striated occurs in abundance at Calderitas and in its finest form is limited to southern Quintana Roo, although it bears close resemblances to Tancah Striated. It is a Classic ware and probably runs the whole length of the Classic Period. The following description is based on a type sample from Calderitas.

Form. The ware seems to come entirely in jars, usually low-necked, heavy vessels evi-dently of large size although no restorable examples were found. Rim forms are complex but fall into two basic types (see fig. 11,b,1-6,9,10, and 7,8,11,12). Necks run from 3 to 8 cm in height, and vessel walls just below the neck from 5 to 10 mm in thickness. No handles, lugs, or supports are associated definitely with this ware; in fact, no basal sherds at all were recovered, in spite of the large sample collected, and so basal associations are unknown.

Surface. The ware is unslipped and unburnished. Most of the sherds are buff, but small per-centages of smoky black, pale orange, and even a few brick-red sherds occur in all samples. The entire exterior body of the jars was covered by striated or raked designs starting just below, or exactly at, the neck-shoulder junction. Design occurs as parallel lines, usually diagonal to the axis of the vessel, running in zones in different directions.

Paste. Paste is coarse in most sherds, medium in a few; temper is large white grit, prob-able calcitic in origin. The ware is moderately hard as Yucatecan wares go, and it fractures with a clean sharp break. Paste color runs to practically all shades of brown—tan, reddish brown, cof-fee, and medium and dark brown being common—and a few sherds show black or even brick red. Color in the paste and surface is in general even and well controlled.

Calderitas Fine Paste Striated (fig. 11,c)

Calderitas Fine Paste Striated is a minor ware found only at the site of Calderitas.

Form. Only a single form occurs in this ware, a flattened-lip double-mouthed jar, one of the mouths evidently being placed vertically on top of the vessel and the other on the shoulder.

Surface. Surface color is very uniform but restricted to yellow buff and dirty white; the sur-face is smoothed but unburnished. Though the ware is unslipped, it possibly has a wash, as surface and paste colors diverge sharply. The exterior surface from a few centimeters below the lip is decorated by belts of intersecting fine, meticulously made striations in sets of 3 to 6 lines or by complete over-all striations running at right angles to each other in definite zones. Striations are much more carefully made (probably with a fine-tooth comb) than in Calderitas Striated.

Paste. The paste shows extremely uniform and well controlled firing, is of fine texture with little deviation, but with a high percentage of temper, is moderately hard, and runs generally to cinnamon brown.

Calderitas Red (fig. 11,d)

As far as my survey shows, Calderitas Red is limited to southern Quintana Roo and runs through the Late Classic Period. The forms are very different from the contemporary Tancah and Coba Red ware in the northern part of the territory, and we recognize an important regional separation here.

Form. Calderitas Red occurs in three basic forms: (1) Comals and plates. Some of these sherds could conceivably go with tall, deep, straight-sided bowls, but the lack of slip on the outer surfaces suggests that they were more probably the form indicated. (2) Simple curved bowls. Some have direct rims with rounded lips, others prominent beveled bolsters; this is the most common of the three types. (3) Jars of a rare form, with fairly high neck for the size of the vessel, and generally slightly bolstered rim. No handles or supports were found in association with this ware, and the few bases collected were all flat or slightly convex.

Surface. The color is uniformly pale buff-orange to straight buff, more commonly the former. It is unburnished but smooth and dusty to the touch. Firing in general is very well controlled, as surface and paste color indicates. All sherds definitely ascribed to this ware are at least partly slipped, with colors running generally to reds, of which the 7.5R hues 4/6 and 4/8 and 2.5YR 5/6 and 5/8 are closest, but some sherds carry orange or brown slips. Slips are very fragile and flaky, and a large proportion of sherds have completely lost the original slip or show only traces of it. The surface is only slightly polished. Direct rim bowls are slipped all over, bolstered rim bowls and comals generally only on the inside, and jar rims may have the slip on either the outside or inside of the neck only. Decoration other than slipping is very rare; it includes punctate and fine line incision.

Paste. In general this is a ware of fine-textured paste with considerable range, running from very fine to medium fine. Paste color runs to dark red-browns and yellow-browns and buff.

Calderitas Polychrome (figs. 11,e; 15,m)

At Calderitas was found in abundance a ware of which only a few sherds occurred at Tancah. It evidently had polychrome designs, but the paint is often badly weathered and many sherds show no traces of it. In view of its virtual chronological (Late Classic) and spatial limitation to the Calderitas site I set up a separate ware classification in the laboratory. Actually it is identical to Thompson's (1939) San Jose IV red-and-black-on-white, to his (1940) polychrome with whitish background at Benque Viejo, and to Smith's (1955) Tepeu 2 Red-and-black-on-cream. Not having seen any of the sherds from these collections I do not know whether Calderitas Polychrome is a separate ware or not. Smith in personal communication would rather not define it as a separate ware. At Calderitas, however, it evidently was made locally, as it is relatively abundant, and for the present, especially in view of its spatial and temporal limitation in the Territory, I will use the ware designation Calderitas Polychrome. Furthermore, some of the forms that are not found outside of Calderitas are obvious copies of forms of the local red slipped ware.

Form. This ware includes chiefly basal break bowls, of which one restorable vessel was found (figs. 11,e,19; 15,m) and a good sample of representative rims. It also includes a few hemispherical bowls with beaklike rims, which duplicate in form those of Calderitas Red, and rarely jars, of which only a few sherds have been found. Of interest is the occurrence with this ware of ringstand bases, but most vessels seem to have had convex or flat bases. The basal break bowls differ from the Yucatan Slate and Tulum Red forms in the nearly vertical walls.

Surface and Decoration. The base clay is smoothed but not burnished, and is generally a very pale orange although buff and creamy gray are also common. Usually one side of the vessel, more often the outside, is left unslipped, and the other side has a dull, almost matte black slip. In most vessels the black is extended to the exterior for 1 cm below the lip. The outer surface may be given a fragile creamy white slip that is used as a base for painted designs in red, orange, and brown. Paints are fragile and rarely well enough preserved for the design to be interpreted.

Paste. Paste is generally of fine to medium texture and moderately hard. A great variety of oranges and reds occurs, but individual sherds are uniform in color.

Calderitas Polished Black (fig. 11,f)

Paste and surface finish indicate this to be a variant of Calderitas Polychrome, but it is distinctive in form, slip, and decorative treatment. Vessels are high, vertical-wall, vase-like forms; they are covered by an over-all well polished black slip and are decorated with wide, shallow, parallel grooves, applied either vertically or horizontally.

Calderitas Heavy Plain (fig. 11,g)

At Calderitas were found a few sherds of an unslipped ware very similar in paste, surface texture, and color to eroded Calderitas Red ware, but distinctive in the great thickness of rim and wall and in the size of the vessels from which they came. Some of the rims are 5 to 6 cm thick, and the body wall just below the rim often has a thickness of 2 cm. Most of the body sherds average well over 1 cm thick. I have tentatively separated these sherds as a separate ware, which I am calling Calderitas Heavy Plain.

10. APPENDIX B ARCHITECTURE

TANCAH

In the course of the survey and excavations at Tancah five new shrines and temples were discovered hidden in the bush west of the two groups mapped by Lothrop.

To the west of Group B is a large rectangular area which lacks architectonic features of either the residential or the religious type. It is bordered to the west and north by low corral-like stone walls, except in the northwest and southwest corners, each of which is occupied by a large platform (Structures 51 and 42) surmounted by one small temple and an altar-like platform (fig. 1). The enclosed space probably served as a plaza or square for ritual activities, and the whole must have formed a related complex with Group B. Ceramic samples collected from the vicinity of the two platforms show close similarity to those from Plaza B, and the buildings probably belong to the same general time span.

Structure 51 is a huge, low platform having a total length of at least 80 m and an undetermined width. On the south side it is easily defined, as it is built to a height of 2 m and faces low ground. Northward, however, it merges with higher rocky terrain and its definition is less clear. On the south it has remains of a small inset stairway (fig. 1). On top of this platform and situated approximately 6 m in from its south edge are the remains of a badly preserved little shrine (Str. 50) of a unique type (figs. 3,b; 12,c,d).

Structure 50 resembles the Temple of the Four Directions (fig. 13,g-i) from Punta Islote on Cozumel Island in having a corbeled vault and four doors, one on each side of the building. Instead of an inner, older temple, however, this structure has in the center of the floor a solid masonry pier approximately 1 m square from which the arches spring. Paired arches spring from the opposite walls, and there is a typical corbeled roof with capstones. On each side of the central pillar was a shallow niche 0.5 m high and approximately 0.3 m wide. The doorways were approximately 0.7 m wide, and walls were on the average about 0.5 m thick. The shrine is small, measuring about 4 by 4.2 m in plan. It has a slightly domed roof and a two-member rectangular molding. The doorways are of typical east-coast type with inset lintels.

On top of Structure 42, a large platform measuring about 30 m east-west by approximately 20 m north-south, is a small rectangular temple (Str. 44). The platform just east of the temple has a height of 3 m but decreases to only 1 m on the opposite side.

Structure 44 is almost destroyed, only the front wall and a part of the roof of the front room being intact (figs. 3,c; 12,a,b). A long rectangular building measuring 11.2 by 4.7 m, it consists of two narrow parallel rooms, one behind the other, running the length of the building. The outer room is entered by three doorways separated by masonry piers 2 m wide, each doorway being 0.7 m wide. The inner room has three corresponding entrances. The structure has a corbeled roof of two arches, each spanning a room; it has a three-member molding of typical Tancah form, and doorways with inset lintels. The total height of the building is 2.5 m. In front of it is a small altar 3 m square.

On the northern periphery of the site, approximately 200 m north of Group B, is another huge platform, Structure 63, which has a length of 55 m, a width of 40 m, and a maximum height of 1.5 m (fig. 12,e). On top are two small temples, Structures 64 and 65, facing each other 5.5 m apart (fig. 3,e). Both are on the east end of the platform. The larger, Structure 64, is set on a low platform base which is almost on the edge of the main platform. Just south of this larger temple are remains of another small platform, and on the west edge of the main platform remains of still another.

Structure 64 is a typical east-coast shrine measuring 4.8 by 3 m in plan. The single room has a doorway of the inset lintel type which faces west and is 0.9 m wide. The structure has a corbeled roof and a typical Tancah three-member molding. The low platform upon which it stands has an inset stairway facing west. The total height of the building was approximately 2.75 m including its platform.

Structure 65 is very similar in plan but is much smaller, measuring 2.85 by 2 m. The roof and the upper member of the molding are completely gone (figs. 3,e, 12,f). The total height cannot have exceeded 1.75 m.

Rancho Temple. Approximately 1 km southwest of the site of Tancah is an isolated temple which from an architectural point of view is one of the most interesting ruins on the east coast. The temple, which I have named the Rancho Temple, after a near-by cattle ranch, is a small masonry building set on a low substructure (figs. 3,d; 12,g-i). The substructure stands approximately 1.25 m high and measures 8.75 m east-west by approximately 9 m north-south. The last measurement is a calculated guess, since the entire north edge has caved in. On the south side is a centered stairway with five steps and balustrades. The stairway juts outward from the platform.

On top of the platform is a fairly well preserved building. It consists of an inner room which may have been a complete structure in itself, predating the final structure as it stands today and having its own vaulted roof and molding. An altar against the back wall occupies most of the floor space. This inner building has a two-member rectangular molding and except for the back wall is perfectly preserved. After this earlier construction, corridors were added on the south, east, and west sides, completely enclosing the earlier structure and converting it to an inner shrine. The complete unit is some 7.5 m east-west by 5.2 m (approximately) north-south, and has a total height of 3.25 m excluding the platform under it. The temple has a single doorway on the south 1.25 m high which had traces of a wooden lintel inset in typical east-coast fashion.

Of great interest is the roofing technique of the building. The inner structure is roofed by a half corbeled vault, which suggests the possibility that it may never have stood alone as a separate building. The front or south corridor has a higher, complete corbeled vault. The roof over the two side corridors has caved in, and what is left indicates that, in part at least, it had a wooden beam and masonry roof similar to those from Tulum. A series of large beams were evidently placed the long length of the corridor at about the level of the second rectangular molding (counting from the roof downward). Over these were laid smaller logs crosswise, and then the whole was topped with a cap of masonry some 0.1 m thick. In the southeast corner of the building the impressions of the logs can still be seen in the masonry above the capstone at the east end of the front corridor arch. The big logs were evidently laid at a point some 0.2 m above the capstone, and the small logs were inserted in the masonry near the roof. The entire roof and east wall of the east corridor have fallen in several large monolithic fragments, attesting to the remarkable tenacity of east-coast mortar. In these fragments may be seen the impressions of the original beams.

The entire back wall has fallen in two huge fragments, molding and all, so that the skill of the Maya in lime masonry can be well observed. The condition of the back, east, and west walls makes complete analysis of the roofing technique difficult without excavation.

The molding is unique in that it has three rectangular and one triangular members. The total height of the molding is about 1.4 m.

The use of beam-and-masonry roofing and the types of molding suggest a Tulum Period dating for this isolated structure. The small ceramic sample dug from a trench along the south edge of the platform, most of it Tulum Buff Paste Censer ware, supports this dating.

ICHPAATUN

Approximately 4 days were spent trenching at this site for stratigraphic materials. In the course of the work a few architectural notes were taken which are summarized below. Escalona Ramos (1946, pp. 522-530) has already given a detailed description of the site, and the notes below are meant as minor additions to his data.

The Great Wall closely resembles in its construction the walls around Tulum (Lothrop, 1924, pp. 68-74) and Mayapan (Shook, 1952). It consists of piled-up chunks of limestone with an outer facing of roughly squared blocks, no mortar being used in its construction. From the inner side it has a general height of 2 to 2.5 m, from the outside somewhat higher, and the breadth runs generally from 4 to 5 m. Traces of a parapet run along the top outer edge, 0.3 m high and 1 m wide. The only entrance in the wall is on the west side, where there is a gateway 0.7 m wide with three or more steps leading up to the passage; it is not roofed today but may have had a Tulum style capstone over the entrance.

In size and shape of drums, columns at Ichpaatun are more like those from Mayapan than those from Chichen Itza. The average drum is 0.7 to 0.8 m in diameter, and 0.2 m deep, and is only roughly tooled. Evidently the masons relied on a thick coating of plaster to give a smoothly rounded contour to the column.

In the course of trenching at the Edificio de Las Grandes Columnas the main or east stairway was uncovered. It evidently had six treads or steps, which are somewhat unusual in that risers are but 0.25 m high and the treads 0.5 m broad, the lowest step having a tread of 0.85 m.

11. APPENDIX C   MISCELLANEOUS ARTIFACTS

Spindle Whorls (fig. 11,i)

Spindle whorls seem to be limited entirely to the Tulum Period. Thirty-one complete whorls were collected during the course of the two field seasons, of which 19 were from Ichpaatun, 11 from Tulum, and 1 from Monte Bravo. The only incised whorl was the one from Monte Bravo. Two whorls, one from Tulum, the other from Ichpaatun, have dark brown slips; all others are buff paste, unslipped and undecorated. Whorls fall into seven distinct forms. Of those shown in figure 11,i, 2, 3, 6, and 7 occur both at Ichpaatun and Tulum, and 4 and 5 are limited to Ichpaatun; the one Monte Bravo example is figure 11,i,8. Approximately half the sample are of the form shown in figure 11,i,7.

Net Sinkers

Of interest at Tulum is the abundance of sherds trimmed into rough rectanguloid objects with grooved ends. Their purpose is problematical, but R. E. Smith suggests in personal communication that they may have been net sinkers or some other type of weight used in fishing. They occur rarely at Mayapan but on the east coast are common in all Tulum Period sites, especially at Tulum. Most examples are of Tulum Red Ware.

Obsidian (fig. 19,b,3-5)

Obsidian seems to be primarily a Tulum Period tool-making medium. In all, 5 obsidian blades were collected after 6 weeks of trenching at Tancah. Neighboring Tulum produced 66 obsidian blades, 3 cores, and 1 arrow point tip. Ichpaatun, also of the Tulum Period, produced 106 blades, 1 arrow point, 2 cores, and 1 scraper. The 1954 season yielded the following blades of obsidian: Cocal 1, 2; San Miguel, 1; Vista Alegre, 1; Yuukluuk, 1; Solfarino, 1; Chiquila, 1; Tulum, 26.

Chert (fig. 19,a,1-9)

In contrast to obsidian, chert is not concentrated in any one period. Most of the fragmentary or complete artifacts are large, well flaked knives or lance heads. The following complete and nearly complete specimens were found:

Tancah, Trench 9, Level 2: Complete knife blade 14 cm long, white
Tulum, S. P. Trench 6: Complete knife blade, 11 cm long, dirty white
Tulum, Trench unknown: Squat point, 6 cm long, 5 cm wide at base, translucent medium brown
Cancun, Group 1: Fragment of knife blade, including the base, 6 cm long, white
Ichpaatun, Trench 2, Level 1: Lower or basal half of knife blade, 5 cm long, translucent brown
Ichpaatun, Trench 2, Level 1: Scraper, gray
Ichpaatun, Trench 3, Level 1: Knife blade, 12.5 cm long, medium brown
Ichpaatun, Trench 3, Level 2: Complete knife blade, 9.5 cm long, translucent light brown

The remainder of the chert was in the form of flakes, and they were rare.

Ground and Polished Tools (fig. 19,a,10-19)

Metates and Manos. At Tulum several fragments of legged metates and of manos were picked up in the trenches along Structure 54.

Celts. These were very rare in the excavations. One complete specimen was collected at Kantunil Kin, and fragments of two others were found at Tulum and Ichpaatun.

Bark Beaters. Two specimens of bark beaters were collected from trenches at Ichpaatun and Tulum.

Ornaments (figs. 11,i,1; 19,b,1,2,6-23)

Practically all ornaments collected during the two seasons were small objects, mostly beads. Shell, jade, and serpentine seem to have been favored materials. The following finds were recorded.

Punta Islote. About half our beads came from trenches at this small site. The sample includes mostly shell beads of two kinds. One is the typical Mesoamerican tubular bead ranging in length from 1 to 2 cm; the other is bow shaped, long, and with trianguloid cross section, and is about 6 cm long. The beads are perforated lengthwise from end to end. Characteristic of beads of either shape is longitudinal banding in red and white. Besides shell, tubular and round beads of jade and of an unidentified brown stone occurred in the same trenches.

The other ornaments recovered during both seasons are listed below:

Tulum
    Trench 4, Level 1   Dark red stone, round bead
    Trench 10   Jade, round bead
    Trench 17   Jade, tubular bead
    Trench 35   Red and white banded shell, 10 small round beads.
                                        Jade, tubular bead
    Trench 45   Shell, incised disk (fig. 19,b,17)

Tancah
    Trench 1, Level 4   Yellow stone, round bead
    Trench 1, Level 5   Shell, 3 small perforated disks with incised designs
    Trench 7   Serpentine, fragment of polished ornament

Miscellaneous Sites
    Kantunil Kin   Jade, large doughnut-shaped bead 3-cm diameter,
                                        perforation 2 cm (fig. 19,b,12)
    San Miguel   Shell, bow-type bead (fig. 19,b,20)

12. REFERENCES

BERLIN, HEINRICH
    1956   Late pottery horizons of Tabasco, Mexico. Carnegie Inst. Wash., Pub. 606, Contrib. 59. Washington.

BRAINERD, GEORGE W.
    1941   Fine orange pottery in Yucatan. Rev. Mex. de Estudios Antropol., 5: 163-83. Mexico.
    1951   Early ceramic horizons in Yucatan. In The civilizations of ancient America, pp. 72-78. Selected Papers 29th Internat. Cong. Americanists. Chicago.
    1956   Changing living patterns of the Yucatan Maya. Amer. Antiquity, 22: 162-64. Salt Lake City.

BULLARD, WILLIAM R., JR.
    1952   Residential property walls at Mayapan. Carnegie Inst. Wash., Dept. Archaeol., Current Repts., no. 3. Cambridge.
    1954   Boundary walls and house lots at Mayapan. Carnegie Inst. Wash., Dept. Archaeol., Current Repts., no. 13. Cambridge.

CHAMBERLAIN, ROBERT S.
    1948   The conquest and colonization of Yucatan, 1517-1550. Carnegie Inst. Wash., Pub. 582. Washington.

ESCALONA RAMOS, ALBERTO
    1946   Algunas ruinas prehispánicas en Quintana Roo. Bol. Soc. Mex. de Geog. y Estad., 61: 513-628. Mexico.

FERNANDEZ, MIGUEL ANGEL
    1945   Exploraciones arqueológicas en la Isla Cozumel. Anales Inst. Nac. de Antropol. e Hist., 1: 107-20. Mexico.

FORD, JAMES A.
    1949   Cultural dating of prehistoric sites in Viru valley, Peru. Amer. Mus. Nat. Hist., Anthropol. Papers, vol. 43, pt. 1. New York.

GANN, THOMAS
    1900   Mounds in northern Honduras. Bur. Amer. Ethnol., 19th Ann. Rept., pt. 2, pp. 655-92. Washington.

LIZARDI RAMOS, CÉSAR
    1939   Exploraciones arqueológicas en Quintana Roo. Rev. Mex. de Estudios Antropol., 3: 46-53. Mexico.

LOTHROP, S. K.
    1924   Tulum: an archaeological study of the east coast of Yucatan. Carnegie Inst. Wash., Pub. 335. Washington.

MUNSELL, A. H.
    1929   Book of color. Baltimore.

NOGUERA, EDUARDO
    1940   Cerámica de Quintana Roo. Mexico Antiguo, 5: 9-40. Mexico.

RELACIONES DE YUCATAN
    1898-1900   In Collección de documentos inéditos relativos al descubrimiento, conquista y organización de las antiguas posesiones españolas de ultramar. 2d ser., vols. 11, 13. Madrid.

RICKETSON, OLIVER G., JR., and EDITH B.
  1937   Uaxactun, Guatemala: Group E—1926-1931. Carnegie Inst. Wash., Pub. 477. Washington.

ROYS, RALPH L.
  1943   The Indian background of colonial Yucatan. Carnegie Inst. Wash., Pub. 548. Washington.

SANDERS, WILLIAM T.
  1955   An archaeological reconnaissance of northern Quintana Roo. Carnegie Inst. Wash., Dept. Archaeol., Current Repts., no. 24. Cambridge.

SHOOK, EDWIN M.
  1952   The great wall of Mayapan. Carnegie Inst. Wash., Dept. Archaeol., Current Repts., no. 2. Cambridge.

SMITH, ROBERT E.
  1955   Ceramic sequence at Uaxactun, Guatemala. Tulane Univ., Middle Amer. Research Inst., Pub. 20. 2 vols. New Orleans.

STEPHENS, JOHN L.
  1843   Incidents of travel in Yucatan. 2 vols. New York.

THOMPSON, J. ERIC S.
  1939   Excavations at San Jose, British Honduras. Carnegie Inst. Wash., Pub. 506. Washington.
  1940   Late ceramic horizons at Benque Viejo, British Honduras. Carnegie Inst. Wash., Pub. 528, Contrib. 35. Washington.

THOMPSON, J. ERIC, HARRY E. D. POLLOCK, and JEAN CHARLOT
  1932   A preliminary study of the ruins of Cobá, Quintana Roo, Mexico. Carnegie Inst. Wash., Pub. 424. Washington.

TOZZER, ALFRED M.
  1941   Landa's relacion de las cosas de Yucatan. Papers Peabody Mus. Harvard Univ., vol. 18. Cambridge.

WINTERS, HOWARD D.
  1955   Excavation of a colonnaded hall at Mayapan. Carnegie Inst. Wash., Dept. Archaeol., Current Repts., no. 31. Cambridge.

MAP OF TANCAH
(Groups A and B from S K Lothrop, 1924)

GL 1-26 GRID LINES
Str 1-70 STRUCTURE NUMBERS
TR 1-15 STRATIGRAPHIC TRENCHES
1-182 SETTLEMENT PATTERN TRENCHES

    × Yield less than 25 sherds
    ○ Yield 25-50 sherds
    • Yield 50-100 sherds
    ▲ Yield over 100 sherds

Fig. 1—MAP OF TANCAH

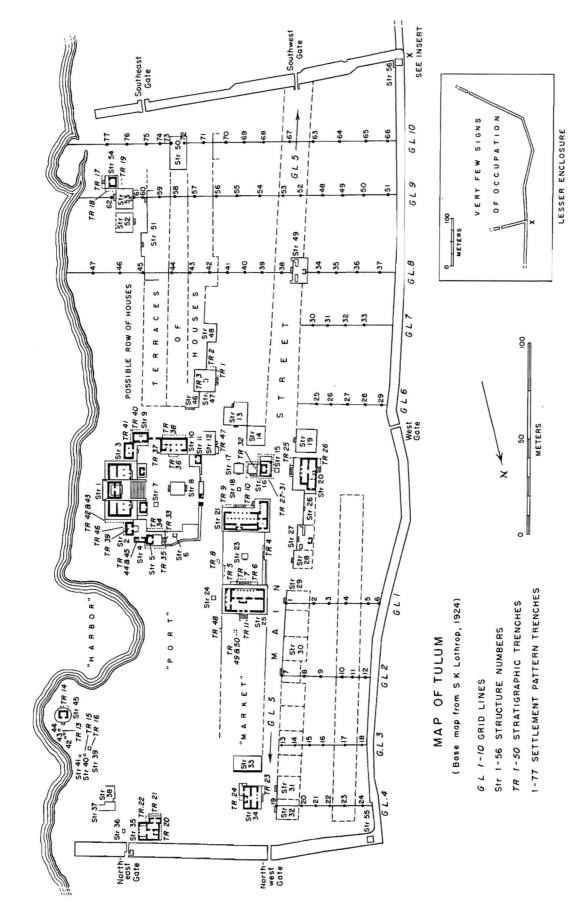

MAP OF TULUM

(Base map from S K Lothrop, 1924)

G L 1-10 GRID LINES

Str 1-56 STRUCTURE NUMBERS

TR 1-50 STRATIGRAPHIC TRENCHES

1-77 SETTLEMENT PATTERN TRENCHES

Fig. 2—MAP OF TULUM

Fig. 3—BUILDING PLANS AND SITE PROFILES

a-f: TANCAH. a: Structure 17, showing architectural details revealed by trenching. b: Structure 50. Plan, elevation, and cross section of small shrine. c: Structure 44. Plan, elevation, and cross section of temple or possibly priests' dormitory. d: Rancho Temple. Plan, elevation, and cross section. e: Structures 64, 65. Temple and small shrine facing each other on top of large platform. Plans, elevations, and profile (64 only). f: Details revealed by trench south of stairway of Structure 55. Profile at top; plan at bottom.

g: TULUM. Three site profiles along Grid Lines 2, 8, 9 to show residential terraces.

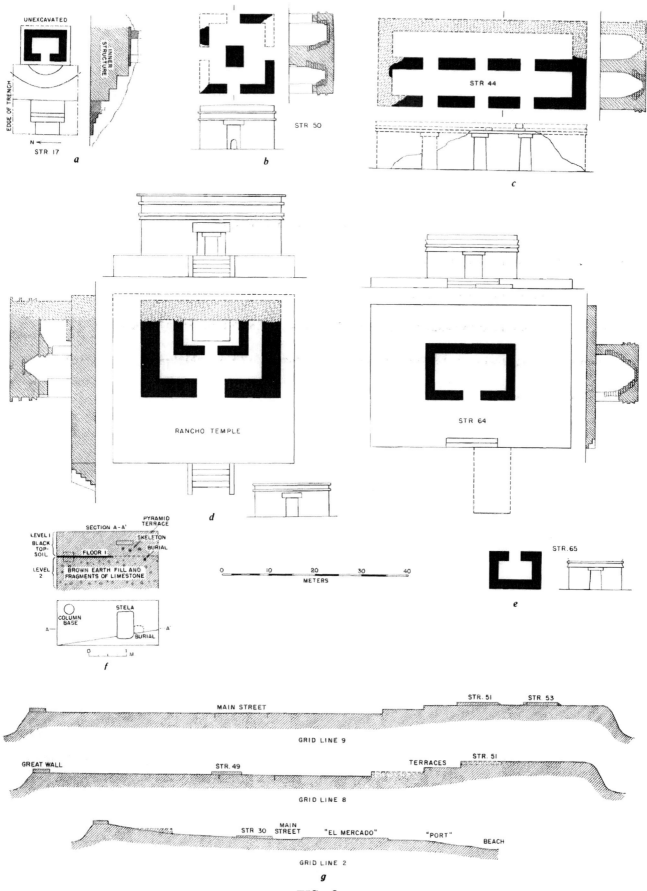

UNEXCAVATED

EDGE OF TRENCH

INNER STRUCTURE

N

STR 17

a

STR 50

b

STR 44

c

RANCHO TEMPLE

d

STR 64

STR.65

e

SECTION A-A'

PYRAMID TERRACE

LEVEL 1

BLACK TOP-SOIL

FLOOR I

SKELETON

BURIAL

LEVEL 2

BROWN EARTH FILL AND FRAGMENTS OF LIMESTONE

COLUMN BASE

STELA

BURIAL

A

A'

0   1   M

f

0   10   20   30   40

METERS

MAIN STREET

STR. 51   STR 53

GRID LINE 9

GREAT WALL

STR. 49

TERRACES

STR. 51

GRID LINE 8

STR 30   MAIN STREET

"EL MERCADO"   "PORT"

BEACH

GRID LINE 2

g

FIG. 3

Fig. 4—TULUM RED BOWLS

<u>a</u>: Basal break bowls, all Tulum.

<u>b</u>: Basal break bowls, all Ichpaatun.

<u>c</u>: Basal break bowls with basal flanges and Z angles: 1-15 Tulum; 16-27 Ichpaatun.

<u>d</u>: Hemispherical bowls: 1-16 Tulum; 17-31 Ichpaatun. 13-16 molcajetes or chile grinders.

Scale is 1/4.

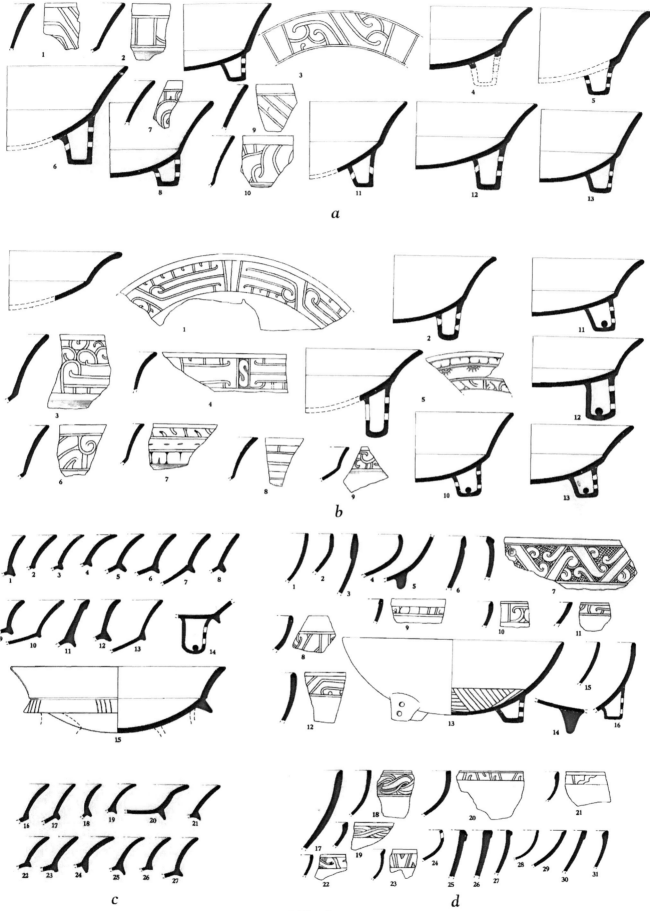

FIG. 4

Fig. 5—TULUM RED JARS AND RARE FORMS

<u>a</u>: Bolstered rim jars: 1-7 Tulum; 8-14 Ichpaatun.

<u>b</u>: Multiple-mouthed jars, all Ichpaatun.

<u>c</u>: Flaring (parenthesis) rim jars: 1-6 Tulum; 7-14 Ichpaatun.

<u>d</u>: Direct rim jars: 1-6 Tulum; 7-17 Ichpaatun.

<u>e</u>: Direct rim incised jars (4 and 13 are bolster rim): 1-8 Tulum; 9-22 Ichpaatun.

<u>f</u>: Rare forms: 1-12 Tulum; 13-17 Ichpaatun; 18, 19 Chiquila (these have coarse paste and are possibly slipped censer ware rather than Tulum Red; 18 may be from annular base rather than rim).

Scale is 1/4.

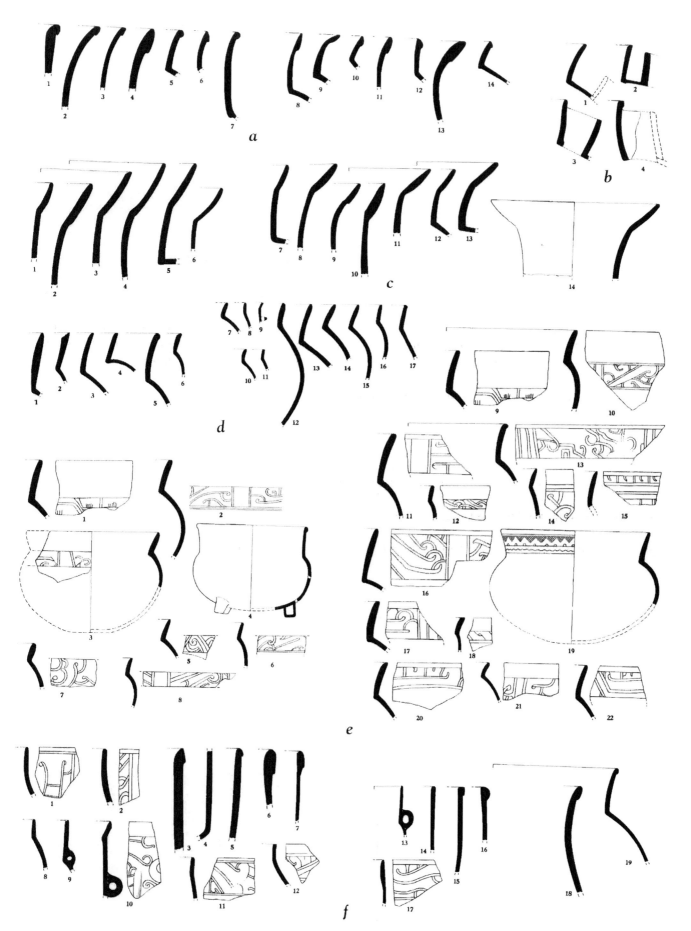

FIG. 5

Fig. 6—TULUM RED AND TULUM PLAIN WARES

a: Miscellaneous Tulum Red sherds: 1-22 Tulum (1, 2 incised necks of jars; 3, 4 vertical strap handles; 5-22 supports); 23 Mulchi; 24 Xelha; 25-67 Ichpaatun (25, 26 incised jar shoulders; 27 incised jar rim; 28 jar wall with horizontal loop handle; 29-36 bases and basal angles; 37, 39 neck of multiple-mouthed jar; 38 jar neck with vertical loop handle; 40 jar wall with horizontal strap handle; 41-67 supports [48, 55 Turkish slipper type; 59, 60 slab]).

b: Tulum Plain. Comals and dishes, all Ichpaatun (10, 11 have horizontal loop handles attached to rims).

c: Tulum Plain. Hemispherical bowls: 1-6 Tulum (4 has flat horizontal lug; 5 horizontal handles; 6 pierced horizontal lug); 7-20 Ichpaatun (17, 19, 20 lugs; 18 horizontal handle). Jars: 21-23 Ichpaatun (21, 22 vertical handles; 23 horizontal lug).

d: Tulum Plain. Handled and lugged jars, all Tulum.

e: Tulum Plain. Jars: 1-33 Tulum; 34-63 Ichpaatun; 64 Vista Alegre.

Scale is 1/4.

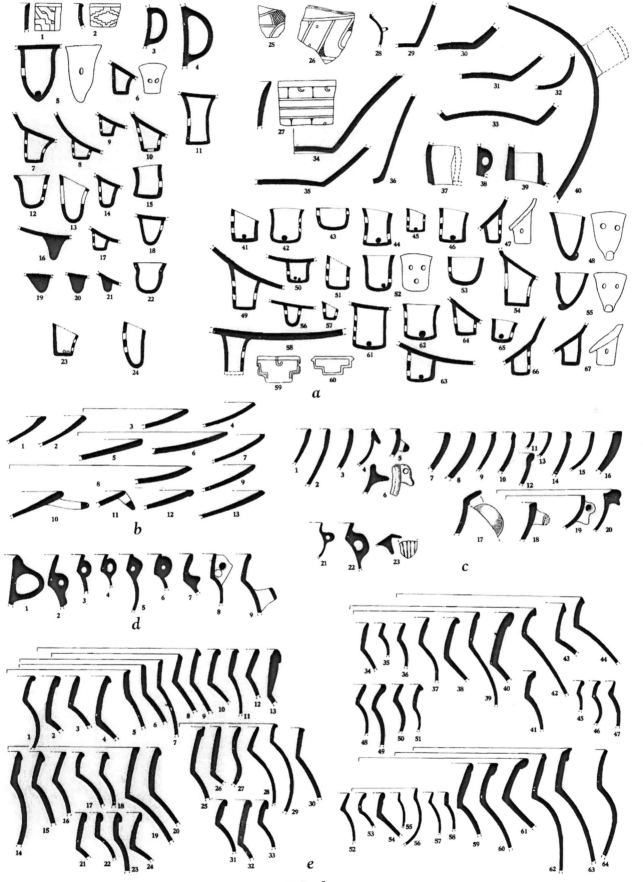

FIG. 6

Fig. 7—TULUM PERIOD WARES

a: V Fine Orange: 1-10 Tulum; 11-14 effigy supports (11 Mulchi; 12-14 Tulum); 15-17 El Meco; 18, 19 Mulchi; 20 Cancun; 21 Vista Alegre; 22 Yuukluuk.

b: Mayapan Black-on-cream: 1-12 Tulum; 13-24 Ichpaatun.

c: Chiquila Censer: 1-21 annular bases and/or rims (1-12 Chiquila; 13-15 Cancun; 16, 17 El Meco; 18-20 Cocal 1; 21 Yuukluuk); 22-54 parts of attached human figures, supports, annular bases, incised and pierced wall sherds (22-38 Chiquila; 39-42 Solfarino; 43, 44 Vista Alegre; 45 Cocal 1; 46, 47 El Meco; 48, 49, 53, 54 Yuukluuk; 50-52 Cancun).

d: Tulum Buff Paste Censer. Rims and/or annular bases: 1-36 Tulum; 37-43 Tancah; 44 Mulchi; 45-48 San Gervasio.

Scale is 1/4.

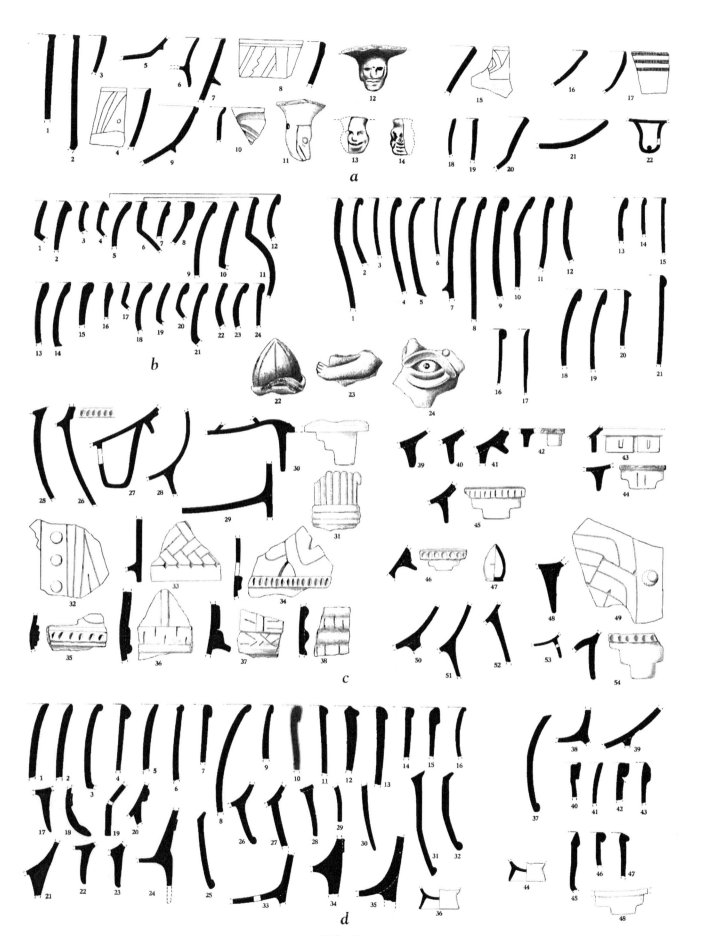

FIG. 7

Fig. 8—TULUM PERIOD CENSER WARES

a: Tulum Buff Paste Censer: 1-9 Tulum; 10 Ak 1; 11 Aguada Grande. See b,30 below.

b: Ichpaatun Censer: 1-29, 32, 33 Ichpaatun (1, 2 whistles; 9 alligator effigy); 31, 34-47 Calderitas. 30 Tulum Buff Paste Censer, Tancah.

c: Ladle censers: 1-3 Ichpaatun; 4 Tulum; 5 Km 14; 6 Chiquila; 7 Tancah; 8 Yuukluuk.

d: Tulum Black Paste Censer: 1, 2 Tulum; 3-5 Punta Islote; 6-8 Ak 1 (8 shark effigy); 9-12 Km 35; 13, 14 Celerain 1.

e: Aguada Grande Censer: 1-13 Aguada Grande (9 possibly Tulum Black Paste Censer).

Scale is 1/4.

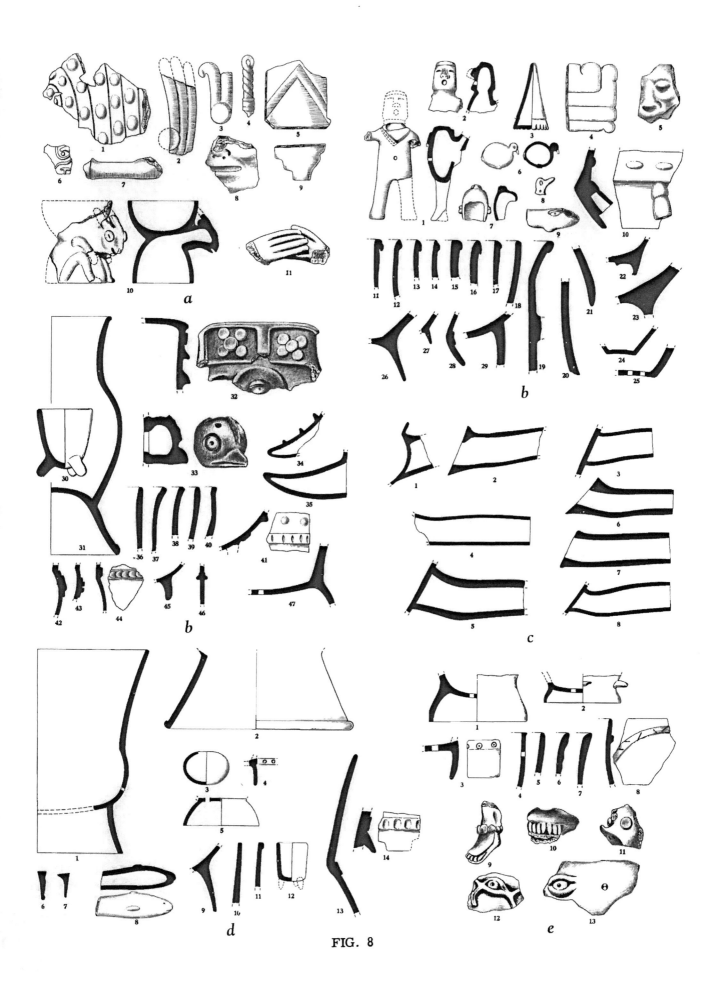

a

b

b

c

d

e

FIG. 8

Fig. 9—VISTA ALEGRE STRIATED AND TANCAH PERIOD WARES

a: Vista Alegre Striated: 1-13 Vista Alegre; 14 Aguada Grande; 15 San Gervasio; 16-20 Tancah; 21-27 San Miguel; 28-30 Monte Bravo; 31, 32 Solfarino; 33, 34 Km 14.

b: Tancah Red: 1-70 Tancah; 71 Santa Maria.

c: Tancah Variegated, all Tancah.

Scale is 1/4.

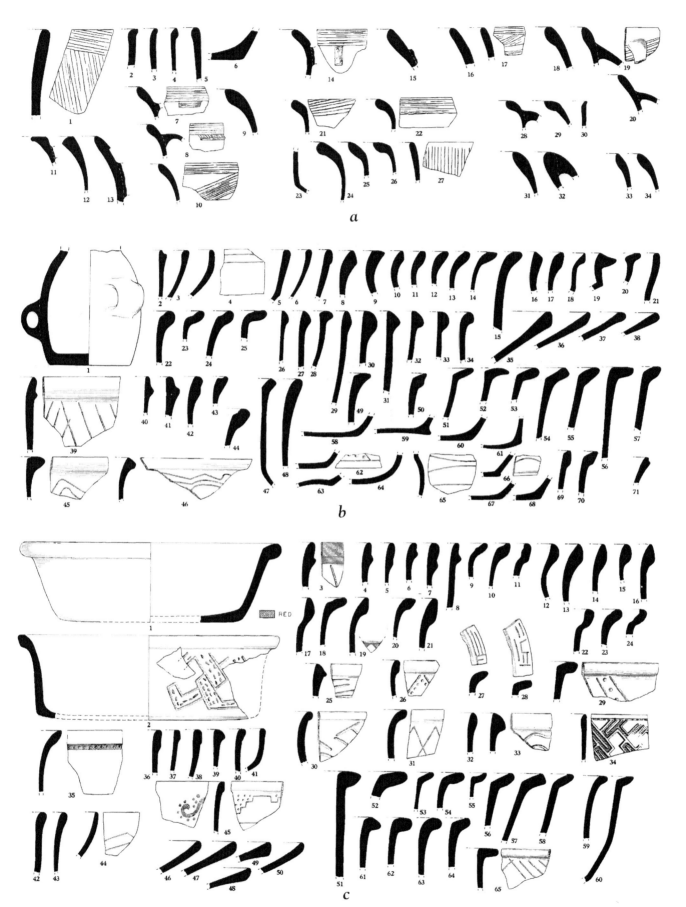

FIG. 9

Fig. 10—TANCAH PERIOD WARES AND REGIONAL POLYCHROME

a: Tancah Variegated, all Tancah.

b: Chiquila Variegated: 1-10 Chiquila; 11-19 Kantunil Kin; 20-22 Km 14; 23, 24 Leona Vicario; 25 El Diez.

c: Restricted orifice bowls (not Vista Alegre Striated; ware like Tancah Striated and Tancah Plain): 1-3 Tancah; 4-6 Kantunil Kin; 7 El Cedral; 8-10 San Miguel.

d: Tancah Plain. Supports: 1, 2 Kantunil Kin; 3 El Diez; 4 San Miguel; 5-7 Tancah.

e: Tancah Striated, all Tancah.

f: Tancah Plain: 1-27 Tancah; 28-30 Xelha; 31, 32 Kantunil Kin; 33 Km 14; 34 Santa Maria; 35-37 Chiquila; 38 El Diez; 39 Monte Bravo; 40 Mulchi.

g: Regional Polychrome: 1-25 Tancah; 26, 27 San Miguel; 28 Calderitas; 29 El Cedral; 30-32 Aguada Grande; 33 Ichpaatun; 34-43 Kantunil Kin.

   Scale is 1/4.

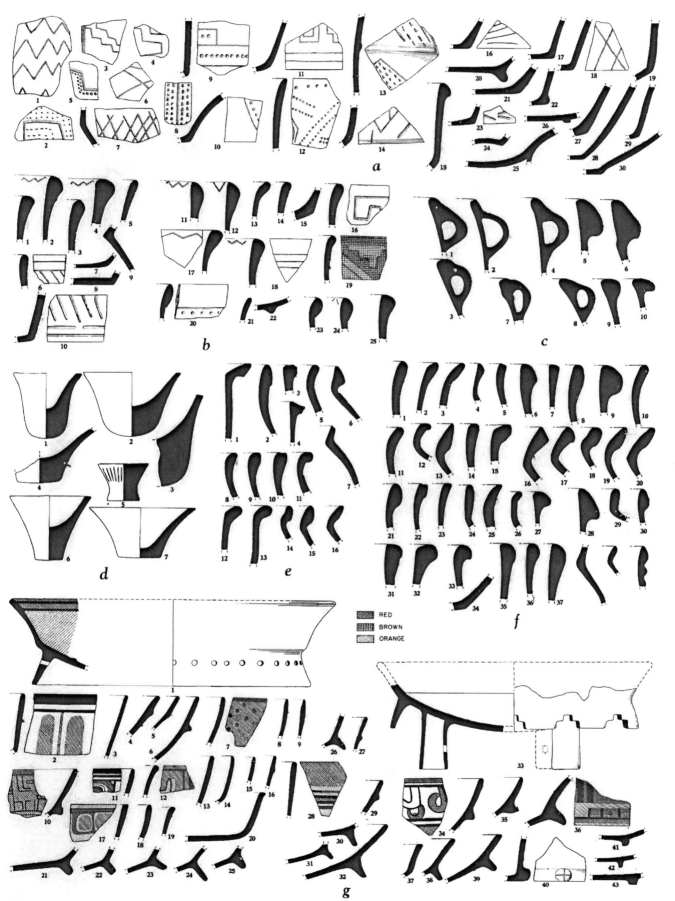

RED
BROWN
ORANGE

a

b

c

d

e

f

g

FIG. 10

Fig. 11—YUCATAN SLATE, CHETUMAL AREA WARES, AND UNCLASSIFIED POTTERY

a: Yucatan Slate (Medium Paste Slate): 1, 2, 25 Km 14 (basal break bowls); 3, 40, 41, 42-49 Tancah (3, 49 basal break bowls; 40, 41 jars; 42-46 basins); 4 El Diez (basal break bowl); 22, 23 Aguada Grande; 24 Xelha (basin); 26-36 San Miguel (26, 27 basins; 28, 29 basal break bowls; 31 jar; 32-36 slab supports); 37, 38 Vista Alegre (slab supports); 39 El Meco (basal break bowl). Thin Slate: 5-14 Tancah; 15-17 Calderitas; 18-21 San Miguel.

b: Calderitas Striated, all Calderitas.

c: Calderitas Fine Paste Striated, all Calderitas.

d: Calderitas Red, all Calderitas.

e: Calderitas Polychrome, all Calderitas.

f: Calderitas Polished Black, all Calderitas.

g: Calderitas Heavy Plain, all Calderitas.

h: Unclassified pottery: 1 Tulum (paste like Tulum Red, over-all brown slip, design outlined by incision and background covered by blue plaster); 2 Leona Vicario (over-all brown slip); 3 Punta Islote; 4 Vista Alegre (red slip exterior, interior plain); 5 Tulum (brick-red paste, over-all gray slip); 6 Tancah (unslipped, with design in red and brown paint); 7, 8 Tancah (over-all black slip); 9 Calderitas (unslipped gray surface); 10 San Miguel (exterior unslipped pale orange, interior purposely smudged black).

i: Shell bow bead: 1 Punta Islote. Spindle whorls: 2, 3, 6, 7 forms at Tulum and Ichpaatun; 4, 5 only at Ichpaatun; 8 Monte Bravo.

    Scale is 1/4.

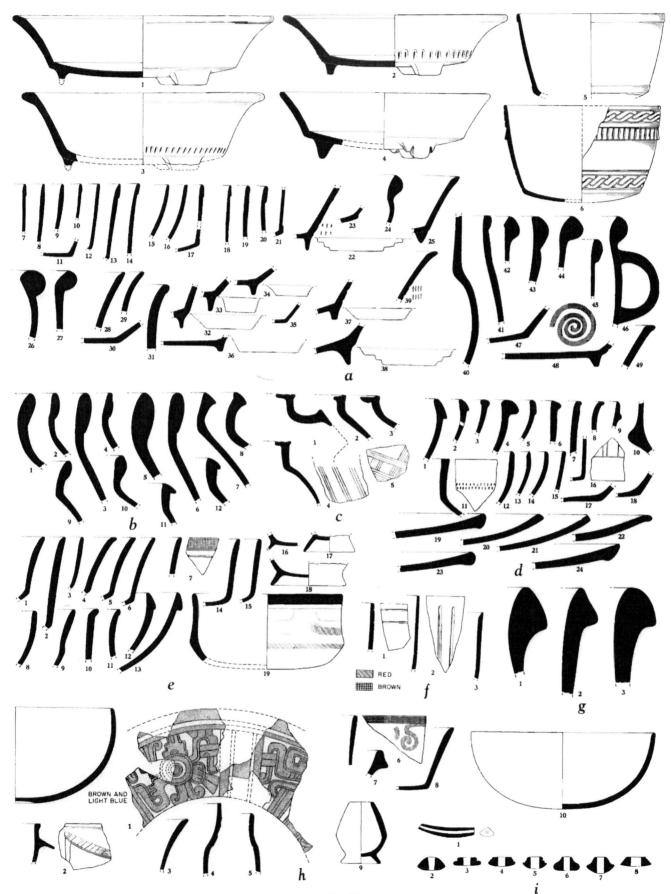

RED
BROWN

BROWN AND
LIGHT BLUE

FIG. 11

Fig. 12—ARCHITECTURE

a-i: Tancah: a,b, Structure 44; c,d, Structure 50; e, Structure 63, platform face; f, Structure 65; g-i, Rancho Temple.

j: Aguada Grande, Temple A.

k: Arrecife Site, Main Structure.

l: El Real, Main Temple.

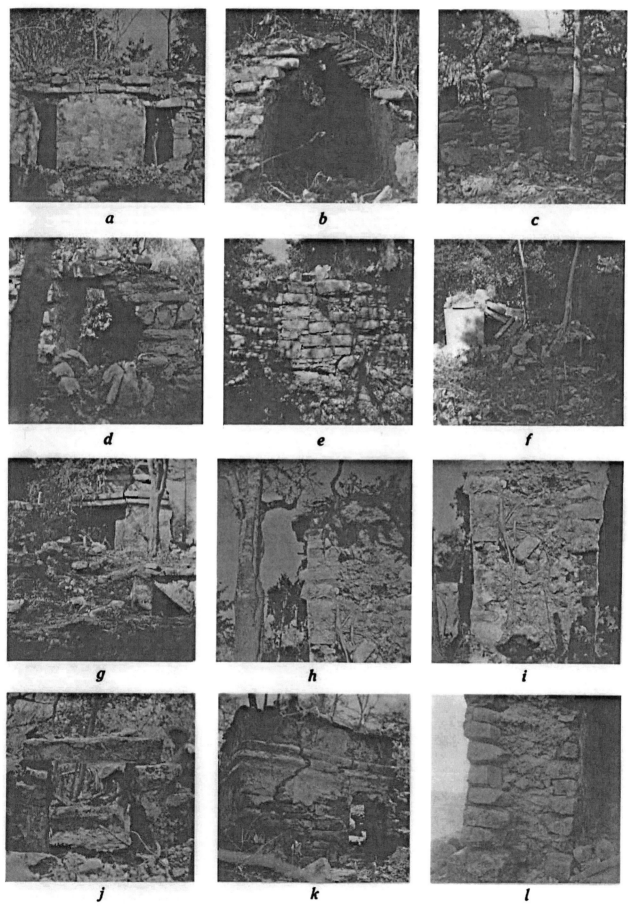

FIG. 12

Fig. 13—ARCHITECTURE, BURIAL, AND GENERAL VIEWS

a-e: Tulum: a, beach which may have served as canoe port; b, Main Street, looking north; c,d, northwest residential zone, as seen from Castillo; e, burial, possibly a human sacrifice (Trench 26).

f,m-o: San Gervasio: f,o, two views of trench through roof and wall debris to floor level in Structure 4, a colonnaded palace; m,n, Structure 3.

g-i: Punta Islote: Temple of the Four Directions, east, south, and west sides, in order.

j: Celerain 2: Isolated shrine of dry stone masonry.

k,l: Arrecife Site: k, view of causeway running from lagoon shore to island upon which site is situated; l, small temple.

FIG. 13

Fig. 14—ARCHITECTURE

a: Janan: Structure 2; note spearhead-like sculptural ornament on roof.

b: Ak 1: Isolated shrine.

c: Caleta of Chakalal: Isolated shrine in background.

d-f: Km 35: d, Temple 1; e, Temple 3; f, Palace (note wooden lintel still in place).

g,h: Palmol: Structure 1: h, idol's throne in upper story.

i: Palmol Playa: Temple 2.

j: Chiquila: Chultun in fill of Great Platform.

k,l: Kantunil Kin: k, Outer Round Platform, after partial excavation; l, Inner Round Platform, after excavation.

m: Ak 2: Isolated shrine.

n: El Diez: Southeast corner of Main Pyramid.

o: Km 14: Structure 2 (pyramid).

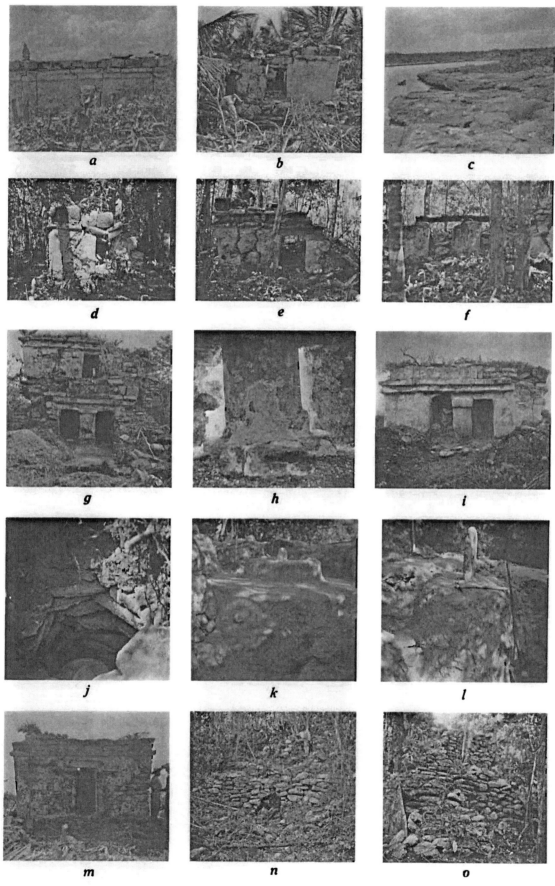

FIG. 14

Fig. 15—POTTERY VESSELS FROM VARIOUS SITES

a-c: Tulum Red basal break bowls: Rim diam. 21.8, 21.3, 19 cm, respectively; Tulum, Ichpaatun, Tulum.

d: Effigy vessel, probably Tulum Red: Ht. 24 cm; Tulum.

e: Tulum Red molcajete or chile grinder: Rim diam. 24 cm; Tulum.

f: Chiquila Censer: Ht. approx. 26 cm; El Meco.

g: Vessel of unknown ware affiliation: Ht. 6.7 cm; Calderitas.

h: Tulum Buff Paste Censer: Ht. 7.3 cm; Tancah.

i: Effigy vessel, probably Tulum Red: Max. ht. 27 cm; Tulum.

j: Tancah Red: Max. ht. 12.4 cm; Tancah.

k: Regional Polychrome, over-all red slip: Rim diam. 16.9 cm; Tancah.

l: Regional Polychrome, over-all orange slipped Z-angle bowl: Rim diam. 49 cm; Tancah.

m: Calderitas Polychrome: Rim diam. 16.4 cm; Calderitas.

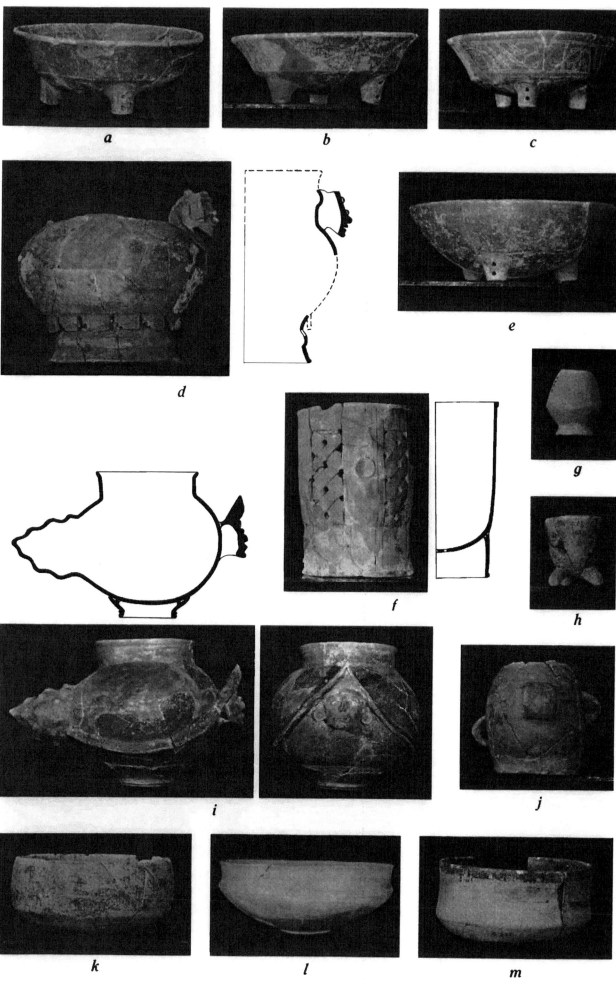

FIG. 15

Fig. 16—FRAGMENTS OF TULUM PERIOD CENSER WARES

a,f,i: Ichpaatun Censer; Calderitas.

b,c: Chiquila Censer; Chiquila.

d: Ware unknown; Las Grecas.

e: Chiquila Censer; Cancun.

g: Tulum Black Paste Censer; Aguada Grande.

h: Tulum Black Paste Censer; Palmol Playa.

j-l: Tulum Black Paste Censer; Tulum.

m,n,p-w: Tulum Buff Paste Censer; Tulum.

o: Chiquila Censer; Tulum.

        Length of b is 15 cm; height of m is 16 cm.

FIG. 16

Fig. 17—ANIMAL AND HUMAN EFFIGIES, AND TUBULAR HANDLED CENSERS

a-e,m,r: Tulum Buff Paste Censer; Tulum.

f-h,o,p,s: Ichpaatun Censer; Ichpaatun.

i: Ware uncertain; Las Grecas.

j: Tulum Black Paste Censer; Km 35.

k: Tulum Black Paste Censer; Aguada Grande.

l,q: Chiquila Censer; Yuukluuk.

n,w,y: Chiquila Censer; Chiquila.

t: Ware uncertain; Solfarino.

u: Ichpaatun Censer; Calderitas.

v: Ware uncertain; Janan.

x: Ware uncertain; Ichpaatun.

Height of n is 8.5 cm; length of y is 17.5 cm.

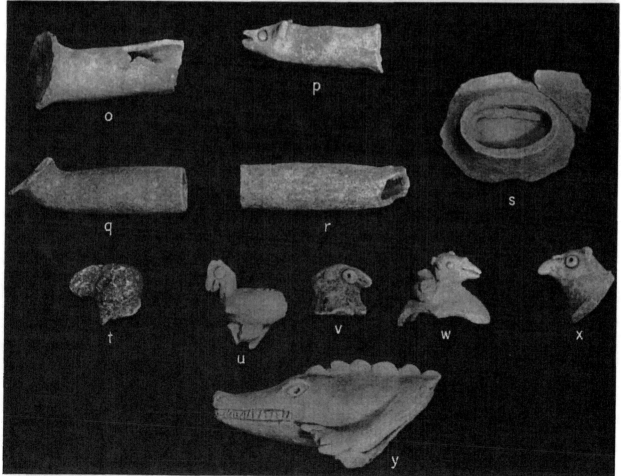

FIG. 17

Fig. 18—TULUM PERIOD POTTERY

a-c: Chiquila Censer: Ht. of a (section) 21 cm; b,c same scale; Chiquila.

d: Chiquila Censer: Max. ht. 24.3 cm; El Meco.

e,f: Tulum Red effigy supports; Ichpaatun.

g-j: Aguada Grande Censer: i,j each 19 cm high; Aguada Grande.

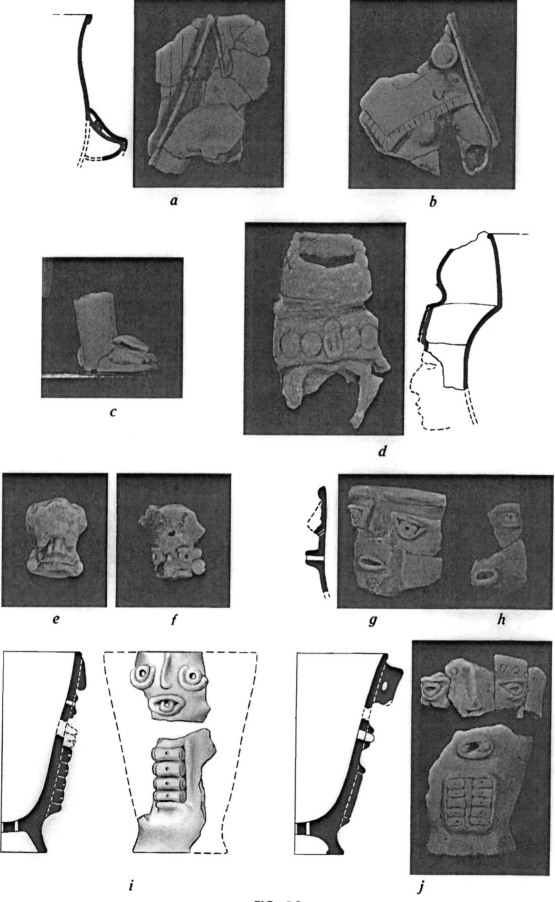

FIG. 18

Fig. 19—ARTIFACTS OF STONE AND SHELL

a: Chipped and ground stone tools: 1-8 chert projectile points; 9 chert scraper; 10, 11 limestone bark beaters; 12, 13 parts of celts; 14, 15 unidentified objects of limestone; 16 metate leg of black volcanic stone; 17-19 hammerstones. 1 Tancah; 2, 10, 15-18 Tulum; 3, 7-9, 11, 12 Ichpaatun; 4 Punta Islote; 5 Cancun; 6 El Meco; 13, 14, 19 Kantunil Kin.

b: Obsidian ornaments: 1 tubular stone bead; 2, 13 shell beads of rectanguloid and bow forms; 3-5 obsidian blades and tools; 6-9, 11, 12 circular stone beads; 10 circular shell bead; 14 ornament (?) of shell; 15, 16 small pierced univalves; 17 incised shell disk; 18 hollow object of bone or antler; 19-23 tubular shell beads. 1, 2, 7, 9, 11, 13, 19, 22, 23 Punta Islote; 3, 4 Ichpaatun; 5, 6, 8, 10, 17, 18 Tulum; 12 Kantunil Kin; 14-16 Tancah; 20 San Miguel; 21 El Real.

Length of a,1 is 14 cm, of b,14 is 9 cm.

a

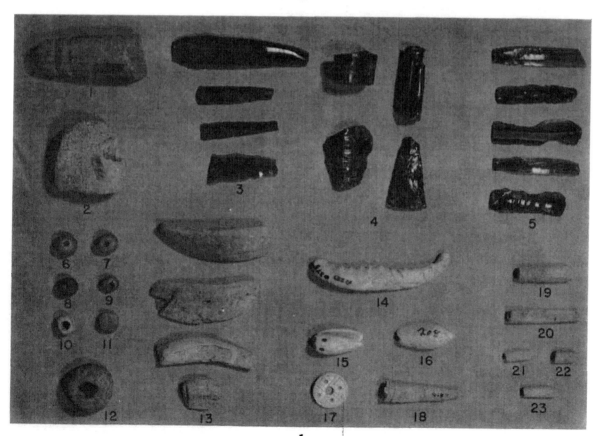

b

FIG. 19

CPSIA information can be obtained at www.ICGtesting.com
Printed in the USA
LVOW09s1929081014

407873LV00024B/637/P